UNLEASHED
& ANOINTED FOR KINGDOM BUSINESS

STACI WALLACE

UNLEASHED and Anointed for Kingdom Business
Published by EMpowerYou Publishing

Copyright © 2018, 2024 by EMpowerYou Publishing
StaciWallace.com

For information, info@StaciWallace.com

Unless otherwise indicated, all Scripture quotations are taken from *The Holy Bible*, New International Version (NIV) ©1973, 1984 by International Bible Society, used by permission of Zondervan Publishing House

All rights reserved
No part of this publication may be reproduced, stored in a retrieval system, or transmitted in any form or by any means – electronic, mechanical, photocopying, recording or otherwise – without prior written permission.

Our books can be purchased in bulk for promotional, educational and business use. Please contact your bookseller or send an email to: info@StaciWallace.com

For booking information visit: www.staciwallace.com
First U.S. Edition: September 2018

Copyright © 2018, 2024 EMpowerYou Publishing
ISBN-13: 978-1-7327916-0-2

ENDORSEMENTS

"I was lost, addicted to the paranormal, homeless, and running from domestic violence when I discovered Staci's books and coaching. I was totally transformed, baptized in the Spirit, set free from bondage, and I now walk in total deliverance personally, financially, and spiritually. My life will never be the same." – *Christina Willis, Certified Coach, Fueled by Fire*

"Staci doesn't just teach from theory, but she lives out the Book of Acts daily, taking Jesus into the marketplace and teaching others how to do the same. Outside of the Bible, this is the most unique book of marketplace evangelism I have ever read."
- *Sean Hyman, Author of The Six Keys to Financial Success and Editor of the Logical Investor, CNBC, FOXnews, FBN, Bloomberg TV*

"We are proud to call Staci and Larry Wallace our friends. The impact they are making in the realm of marketplace ministry is profound. We consider this book a 'how to' guide for those who long to experience the Kingdom outside the walls of the church." – *David & Nicole Binion, Lead Pastors of Dwell Church, Dallas, TX*

"Having known Staci Wallace for more than twenty-three years, I can't imagine a woman more qualified to write a book about being Unleashed and Anointed for Kingdom Business. Most Christians seem to have an on/off switch for the Holy Spirit. It's 'on' when they attend Sunday church services, but 'off' the rest of the week when real life happens. Staci's switch is always 'on' and her heart for evangelism is seen daily in the signs and wonders that follow her life."
- *Terry Toler, Author of The Jesus Diet and How to Make More Than a Million Dollars*

"I have never read a more practical, yet inspiring book about what it means to be empowered by the Holy Spirit in our everyday lives. As a female executive, I am deeply inspired by Staci's boldness in sharing her faith, as well as the miracle stories she has experienced in the marketplace. This book is a tool to equip you to be the Kingdom CEO you are destined to be." – *Karen Imhoff, CEO, Big Easy Shades*

"Before reading this book, I was a mastery level educator weighing 436 pounds, struggling with my identity, health, and finances. I knew 'about' the Holy Spirit, but this book helped me apply the authority of the Kingdom in every area of life. I lost 180 pounds, restored my finances, and am now teaching others about the incredible gift of the Holy Spirit in business and life." – *Christi Morris, M.Ed, Creative Specialist, Epiphany Global*

ACKNOWLEDGMENTS

To My Knight in Shining Armor, Larry:
You inspire me to stretch, soar and continue to scale mountains others deem impossible. You are a quiet giant of great generosity and the most patient and selfless leader I've ever met. The sacrifices you have made on behalf of those we have impacted these past three decades together will only be fully understood on the other side of eternity. I love you forever.

To my Young King, Payton:
You are a mighty wise king and your life is leaving a historical legacy on this generation. Your "1-2-3 BAM" faith inspires me daily to know that God is a miracle working God, and His power is only limited by our belief. Thank you for being a God-chaser and making the Kingdom Way your priority in life and business.

To my Queen Bee, Alexia:
You are my sweet bee with light that radiates from every smile you share. I love the way you love God, defend others, and seek God's Kingdom above all else. God has uniquely prepared you to bring hope, help, and healing to many. Your willingness to touch the untouchable and love the unlovable is your secret sauce in this life. I love you to the sun and back.

To my Momma:
Words will always fail to adequately express the love, respect and honor I have for you as my life-giver. Thank you for being a radiant expression of God's love and an example of His Word. You and Dad proved this UNLEASHED lifestyle before it ever became a book. Thank you for the many hours poured into editing this work. I love you so much and I know Dad is giving us both the thumbs up from Heaven.

To our Fueled by Fire family:
You are turning the words of this book into a marketplace revolution. Thank you for making the sacrifices necessary to reflect God daily and to be the voice of a new generation.

To EMwomen and Epiphany Global Contributors:
You have helped make this book available to thousands of people around the world. This message of the Kingdom must be spread throughout the nations. Thank you for making that possible.

UNLEASHED
& ANOINTED FOR KINGDOM BUSINESS

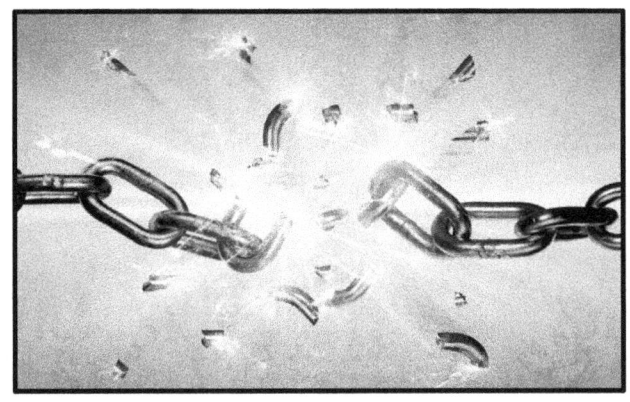

A BLUEPRINT FOR DOING BUSINESS GOD'S WAY

STACI WALLACE

CONTENTS

| | The Beginning | 9 |

Section 1
A NEW AWAKENING

Chapter 1	The Birth of a Revolution	17
Chapter 2	Anointed for Business	27
Chapter 3	The Hustle	35
Chapter 4	Dominion in the Marketplace	41

Section 2
KINGDOM DYNAMICS

Chapter 5	Kingdom Purpose	45
Chapter 6	Kings, Priests and Prophets	49
Chapter 7	Kingdom Mentality	53
Chapter 8	CEO Mindset	57

Section 3
THE REFORMATION BEGINS

Chapter 9	Marketplace Revival	63
Chapter 10	Marketplace Mavericks	67
Chapter 11	Superhero Courage	71
Chapter 12	Heaven on Earth	75

Section 4
TAKING IT TO THE STREETS

Chapter 13	This is War	79
Chapter 14	Embracing Change	83
Chapter 15	Grow Up!	87
Chapter 16	This New Life	93

Section 5
HOLY SPIRIT & YOU

Chapter 17	The Force Awakens	99
Chapter 18	Direct Connect	105
Chapter 19	Spiritual Gifts	111
Chapter 20	Supernatural Communication	119
Chapter 21	The Power Gifts	125

Section 6
LAUNCHING OUT

Chapter 22	The Final Countdown	129
Chapter 23	Healing 101	135
Chapter 24	Break Every Chain	141
Chapter 25	The Jezebel Spirit	147
Chapter 26	Deliverance 101	153

Section 7
THE BLESSED LIFE

Chapter 27	Financial Freedom	161
Chapter 28	Wise Investing	171
Chapter 29	Go and Grow	179

"And these miracle signs will accompany those who believe: They will drive out demons in the power of My name. They will speak in tongues. They will be supernaturally protected from snakes and from drinking anything poisonous. And they will lay hands on the sick and heal them."

– **Mark 16:17-18 (TPT)**

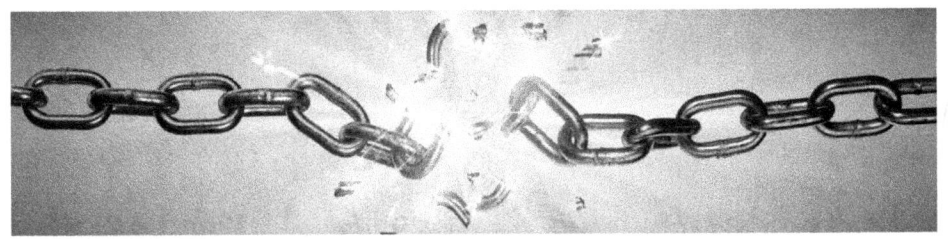

THE BEGINNING

Now is the time for a chosen remnant of God-fearing men and women to UNLEASH the power of the Holy Spirit in their everyday lives.

UNLEASHED (v): to be loosed from bondage; to be sent with great force

It was the summer of 2017 when I began to sense a shift taking place. We had been enjoying an extended season of business success, abundance, and financial freedom. Personally, I had been in a gratifying season of breaking impressive sales records and winning accolades, honors, and awards for my efforts in business. My income and trajectory were so substantial that my husband was able to retire from his high-stress position as COO of a telehealth company in Texas. We were traveling around the world as our business was in 25 countries and I was winning awards, trips, and prizes that allowed us to take exotic vacations almost monthly.

Our ego was fed daily as social media loved following our material-rich lifestyle of the rich and blessed. But then, after a trip to Africa, something began to shift in my spirit. I started to feel a deep hunger for more than what money could buy. I loved our life and lifestyle, but deep in my core…I wanted more. I became extremely unsettled in my spirit but wasn't quite sure what it was or where it was taking us.

Then, in July of 2017, two of my key business leaders in Puerto Rico were recruited to another company that offered them significant financial benefits.

I was happy for them, knowing how they had each grown to become strong leaders and worthy of such financial reward. But what that represented to our business was a potential loss of 60% of our income if we didn't replace them immediately. I had been an integral part of scaling companies into the hundreds of millions and so I was well acquainted with corporate shake-ups and how to make sudden moves to preserve business development.

My initial reaction to the situation in Puerto Rico was to simply put a retention plan in place and begin rebuilding a new leadership team immediately. But while getting ready to head to Puerto Rico, I sensed the voice of the Holy Spirit saying, *"Do not rebuild Puerto Rico. I am about to do a new thing."*

The command seemed crazy considering the significant threat of financial loss could occur. I told my husband what I felt the Holy Spirit was saying and he boldly responded, "Well, I don't want you getting on a plane if God's not in it." We made the decision to obey the voice, not rebuild Puerto Rico, and instead, begin focusing our efforts on our U.S. mainland business growth.

Two months later, we were in a mastermind meeting with 15 other CEO's when I opened my weather app to see a massive hurricane devastate the island of Puerto Rico. My heart broke for the families and businesses of the island. At the same time, I felt a deep sense of peace because I had already heard from God two months earlier. I knew in that moment that He was guiding us into a new season. Hope rushed over me like a massive wave, and despite the concern for our financial needs, I knew God was shifting our focus and attention.

WILL YOU SAY YES?

That was September 2017. Then, in early October, I was awakened at 3:00 a.m. by a new song in my spirit. It was a simple song, but it carried significant weight in what it was asking us to do. The lyrics of the song were:

> *Will you say YES? Will you sacrifice your life?*
> *Will you say YES? Will you raise the knife?*
> *Will you say YES? Or will you turn and walk away?*
> *Will you say YES to me today?"*

That morning, I knew God was making a request of me that would require personal and business sacrifice. What it was, I wasn't sure, but I knew He was asking me to shift my natural thinking to an eternal perspective. Soon, it was clear that God was directing me to make His business my highest priority and to give the rest of my life as a spokesperson for His Kingdom purposes.

It was as if I was being called up for a higher purpose than mere profits or positioning. As I sat in my office, singing the words of that song, I began to dissect each word and realized that it was a calling to a life of sacrifice. I scrolled through Bible stories in my mind that fit the narrative of the song.

Will you say YES? Will you sacrifice your life?
Thoughts of Jesus, suffering on the cross, rolled like a movie in my head.

Will you say YES? Will you raise the knife?
I imagined Abraham raising the knife to offer his beloved son as a sacrifice to God before the ram was heard in the thickets.

Will you say YES? Or will you turn and walk away?
Noah was criticized for being a "crazy" man as he built the ark, but his obedience saved his family and legacy.

The more I thought about the ludicrous "YES" stories in the Bible, I realized that to say "YES" may mean we may have to sacrifice something to follow the call of God. Saying "YES" doesn't always mean being celebrated and cheered. Take it from any former U.S. President, "YES" often means being stretched, ostracized, vilified and even persecuted. What was God asking of me? And why now? I didn't know what it would entail, but at 3 a.m., while sitting at my desk, a fierce boldness rose up in my heart as I confidently said "YES" to whatever He may ask. As I was still in what I knew to be the holy presence of God, I heard God's still small voice say: "To obey is greater than sacrifice." (1 Samuel 15:22)

That was early October 2017, and I knew God was getting ready to shake things up. I began to feel unsettled in my spirit and at what I was witnessing in the Body of Christ at large. A holy anger and unrest began to rise up within me as if suddenly a blinder had been torn from my eyes and I was seeing for the first time. I saw compromise and corruption in our government, in the media, in front-line leaders, in organized religion and worst of all, I recognized a personal apathy, even in my own life.

Then, out of the blue, I received a call from a small group leader in a local mega-church, asking if she could use my first book, *Mission Possible,* for their upcoming Bible study. I was thrilled to say "YES". We hadn't marketed that book in over 10 years, and I was shocked she even knew about it.

She proceeded to ask if I would create a supporting video for her small group to launch the study. One "YES" led to another "YES" and the next thing I knew, I was sitting in my office from morning to sundown, re-reading and devouring my own book. I was transformed from the inside out with words God had given me a decade earlier.

Mission Possible is a book and life mastery course devoted to teaching readers how to hear God's voice and become the courageous leader He has called them to be in the marketplace. Reading my own words, ignited a fire within me. I felt a sudden desire to use the business acumen He had given me over my 30 years of business success to launch a new and ambitious season of marketplace ministry to this generation.

Be careful when you say "YES" to God because, based on my own experience, it will usually lead you to even more levels of sacrifice. I had no idea how saying "YES" to a small Bible study group would awaken a sleeping giant within me to be a bold and outspoken voice of truth to my generation.

On that early morning in October, when I heard that song in my spirit, I had no idea what was about to happen in the landscape of America and what my "YES" would require. I didn't know that governments would become so steadfast against Biblical morality or that they would soon authorize the death of full-term babies in the womb of a mother. I didn't know that the very relevance of scripture would be questioned, and its authority be challenged by an entire generation. And little did I know that a bold and liberal movement of women's equality would become so outspoken and passionately set against the Word of God with a vengeance to see politics win over righteousness.

Suddenly, I could see why God had seasoned me as a communicator and negotiator for 30 years in the marketplace and why He had prepared me, as a businesswoman, with a fierce confidence to stand up as a catalyst of monumental change. I felt God shifting me from the mindset of advocating for corporations into a radical boldness to fight against the diabolical agenda that was so clearly dominating the media and disrupting the spiritual DNA of our nation.

Isaiah 59:19 - *"When the enemy comes in like a flood, the Spirit of the LORD will lift up a standard against him."*

The more I saw women in politics championing marches and media campaigns that directly violate scripture, the more I wanted to speak out for the truth of God's Word. Suddenly, the Holy Spirit began to awaken a dormant dream in my heart that I had buried for an entire decade.

In 2006, my husband, Larry, was growing a start-up technology company with my brother, who had a knack for building very successful corporations. Soon, the start-up team became a massive company and eventually scaled to over a billion dollars. It was surreal to see such growth in so little time. Despite the success they were having, we couldn't deny our hearts for doing something more than creating profits. So, we stepped away from that company to launch EMwomen (EMpowering Women) on 7/7/7 (July 7, 2007) at 7:00 p.m.

EMwomen was a non-profit organization that focused on helping women and girls in need throughout the world. In its prime, EMwomen was feeding over 400 homeless people each weekend, hosting live motivational events, and had launched a social network that was reaching women in 22 countries. But then the financial recession occurred in America and the 2008 economic crisis hit our organization head-on like a hurricane. Our primary donors were crushed by the financial collapse and donations to EMwomen soon dried up. We held on, pouring every penny of our savings into our online social network and events, but our finances ran out, and we could no longer sustain the mission. We were heartbroken over the collapse, knowing that there was still so much to be done in the lives of women throughout the world. We knew the seed had been planted deep in our hearts for the EMwomen vision, but for some reason, God was allowing this shift to occur. We knew we had to allow our dream to go into a cocoon of silence until further notice.

To rebuild our financial reserves, in 2009, I accepted an executive leadership position with a health and wellness company and headed into a decade of success in corporate America. My books, music, ministry and EMwomen were all put on hold as God shifted me into a new season of favor, financial increase, and extraordinary business success.

My husband was also thrust into multiple successful business launches and our ride of increase lasted for another 10 years. Then came the shift in 2017 as we watched the hurricane sweep through Puerto Rico. We knew in our hearts that the storm was not sent to destroy us, but to propel us into a new season of marketplace ministry. We have learned that not every storm is an attack of the enemy. Sometimes God uses wind, rain and pressure to push us into a new season that becomes a set up for even greater abundance.

AWAKEN THE SLEEPING GIANT

We wake up every day to reports of bombings, mass shootings, shifted morality and confused systems of basic ethics. And while we have progressed as a nation in technologies and business innovation, we have digressed as a nation in spirituality, harmony and peace. The clash of good versus evil has never been stronger, and the cry for justice has never been louder.

Now is the time for a chosen remnant of God-fearing men and women to UNLEASH the full potential of God's Spirit against the darkness that has saturated our generation. As business mavericks, entrepreneurs, moms and dads, politicians, and influencers, we can no longer be apathetic to the growing animosity of darkness, perversion, and division that permeates our nation. We cannot sit back in our corner offices of padded perfection and let the world around us continue to decay. Clearly, for things to change, we must change, and God has given us the power, timing, and authority to do so.

While confusion and moral decay seem to be screaming in the ears of our children, there is a growing force of God-chasers who are hungry for a move of God and ready to rise up as catalysts of change in the marketplace and world. Although this book holds powerful prophetic messaging to ALL of God's people, I am fully committed and bound to the call of God, as a female leader, to stand up for God's truth as a woman of faith, liberated and empowered, not by politics or policies, but by the power of the cross, the fullness of the Holy Spirit, and the truth of God's Word.

We are a waking up a generation of sleeping giants, both male and female, young and old, who are ready, willing and able to be the voice of spiritual truth that this generation so desperately needs.

That is why my husband and I were quick to say, "YES" to God's voice and step away from our corporate pursuits to become passionate and fully devoted to marketplace ministry. We know God is shifting kingdoms to bring healing to the nations of the earth. He is about to bring new order to the seven pillars of society including the areas of faith, family, education, government, media, entertainment and business.

TAKING DOMINION

> When God has full control over the assets of your intelligence, experiences, and abilities, you will be able to take dominion in the marketplace, not because of your greatness, but because of the Great One living in you.

The enemy abhors books likes this because it will unleash God's power on earth and resurrect marketplace giants who have fallen asleep with the lullabies of the world's agenda. As you read through the pages of each chapter, let them awaken you to God's miraculous power. Let them teach you to discern His voice so that you will become a fierce, bold, and righteous leader in your workplace and at home. Get ready to intimately know the Holy Spirit of God, and invite Him to be your counselor, advocate, and guide. Then, you will boldly take dominion over any principalities that would endeavor to hold you back.

There is a reason you are reading this book. You KNOW there is more to life than what you are currently getting, and your hunger is driving you to find out how to get it. No matter what your history looks like or what you've had to do to make it here, God is about to use your history to leave a legacy of hope, help, and healing for the world around you.

UNLEASHED and Anointed for Kingdom Business is a "how to" book and course written to give the step-by-step training you need to have supernatural discernment in the boardroom, wisdom in the classroom, compassion at home and the miracle-working power of God in every area of your life. You will receive clear instructions on how to cooperate with your God-given destiny as His conduit of miracles, abundance, spiritual authority, and financial prosperity to the people around you.

This book is not meant to make you comfortable. On the contrary, it was written to disrupt the status quo, awaken your spirit, give you a Kingdom identity, and ignite your passion for taking action so that, together, we can make change happen in this world. You may not realize it, but God has been intricately preparing you for years, "for such a time as this".

The enemy fears the day you become the God-fearing leader of boldness and significance you were destined to be. I assure you that the enemy of your destiny does NOT want you to finish this book, nor does he want you to recognize and fulfill your divine potential.

He could care less if you become successful, climb to the top of your game, gather a mass number of followers, be a notable speaker, corporate executive, make excessive amounts of money or experience fame and fortune. But what scares the HELL out of him, is when you recognize your place in the Kingdom of God on earth and you awaken to God's highest purpose for your life. When that happens, you will fully allow the Holy Spirit of God to flow through you, empower your decisions, and use your life and talents to penetrate the marketplace and make His name great in all the earth.

God wants to use your success for a much higher purpose than making money or storing up wealth. Let this book challenge your thought processes, engage your core values, motivate your passions, and empower you to be *UNLEASHED and Anointed for Kingodm Business*. Your mission field, the marketplace, awaits you. Let the great adventure begin!

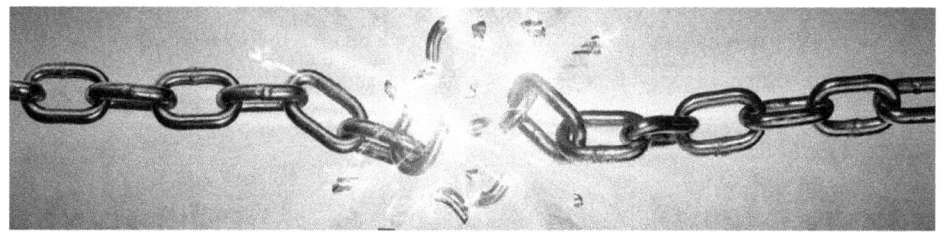

CHAPTER ONE

THE BIRTH OF A REVOLUTION

"Jesus intentionally recruited marketplace people who were not members of the religious establishment because His objective was to create a new social vehicle - the Church, a movement that was meant to be the counterculture rather than the subculture."
- Anointed for Business, Ed Silvoso

Have you ever stopped to consider the magnitude of what Jesus created in three short years? What was the secret sauce behind the sales strategy and marketplace revolution He UNLEASHED on earth? What were the tactics He used that we can apply to our everyday businesses, negotiations, and efforts as leaders? As we examine His business style, you will see the strategic principles Jesus demonstrated that resulted in an explosion of geometric growth like has never been seen in history. His marketing plan resulted in the greatest franchise system of all time. It was a revolution that created the #1 best-selling book since human life began. It gave birth to the Kingdom on earth and empowered the most sustainable messages ever spoken by the most renowned communicators in history. It took God, Himself, stepping into humanity and choosing an unorthodox sales and marketing team of ordinary men and women who created an extraordinary movement that changed the world.

THE ULTIMATE SALESMAN

Jesus was a businessman before He was a rabbi. He was a carpenter in the marketplace before He was known as a miracle worker. He was God in the flesh and an executive leader who knew how to strategically recruit a team of ordinary people from the marketplace that would cause His message to go viral. He quickly set a new standard, different than the norm of temple worship. He empowered both men and women to move fluidly throughout the marketplace and take His mission to the world. He offered us a perfect template on how to launch, lead and leave a legacy by building a great team around a unified message.

> **Jesus was a very different kind of rabbi and spiritual activist. He was an out-of-the-box leader, a culture-shaker, and mindset disrupter.**

Jesus could have chosen the wealthiest, the most impressive in pedigree, the strongest in communication skills or even the most politically correct. But instead, He chose a motley crew of fishermen, business leaders, female-investors, a harlot and everyday entrepreneurs to be the catalyst of the most significant message of all time.

Some saw Jesus as a rebel, while others saw Him as a revolutionary. Rebels merely try to overturn the past while revolutionaries risk all to change the future. To walk with Him, whether male or female, was risky business and those that did so were courageously willing to sacrifice all for the sake of His message. Jesus, the Messiah, Prophet, King, and High Priest came to show us how to birth a revolution that disrupts the status-quo and shakes the foundations of what has become "normal."

Jesus didn't hide behind costly walls of institutions, political offices or temples. Instead, He unleashed God's power in the marketplace, on the streets, and in the homes of ordinary people ready for extraordinary change. Jesus' life was the most exceptional example of how to franchise a message of hope, help and healing that would build a lasting legacy for eternity. Instead of representing temples made by man, Jesus was fluid like water, teaching his followers how to seep into the crevices of society and immerse the marketplace with the Good News of the Kingdom of God.

Luke 4:43 - *But he replied, "I must preach the Good News of the Kingdom of God in other towns, too, <u>because that is why I was sent</u>."*

Jesus came to teach us about how to bring Heaven's culture to earth and how we should live righteous as royal heirs, even in our everyday jobs, homes, and communities. Today, the most significant expansion of goodwill and spiritual enlightenment will not come from church platforms, professional speakers, expensive buildings, high-tech worship venues, or even religious institutions of learning. Instead, it will be birthed through ordinary people who say, "YES" to allowing the Holy Spirit of God to use them at home and in their jobs to UNLEASH the presence of God in their everyday lives and throughout the world.

BEYOND SUCCESS LIES SIGNIFICANCE

As a corporate leader, businesswoman and senior executive, I have experienced, firsthand, the endless struggle of climbing the corporate ladder, searching for fulfillment in my titles, salaries, awards and even in the success of my marriage and my children. Unfortunately, I've also felt the suffering and stress that the pursuit of "more" can yield. Enough never seems to be enough when we are living under the patterns of a world immersed in greed, selfish ambition, high performance, and human power. After reaching the pinnacle of success in my career, I still found myself starving for significance and feeling a lack of fulfillment. What I discovered in my process of liberation and enlightenment has led me to a life of peace and profits that have awakened my spirit, soul, and body. It is from that point of personal transformation that I write the principles of this book.

Whether your primary influence is in a schoolhouse, courthouse, White House, boardroom or within your own house as a stay-at-home mom, God wants to partner with you and empower you to be his eyes, ears, voice, hands, feet, and heart to a lost and hurting generation that is crying out for attention.

We search for purpose in our jobs, talents or professions but we were not born to merely build empires and incomes. The search for success will never fulfill our longing for greater significance. That is the proverbial hole in our heart that can only be filled when we engage our higher purpose.

Today's push for gender equality seems, to many, to be the answer to heal the pain of suffering. But the truth is that equality, though noble and good, is never going to heal our need for greater spirituality.

That is why, as leaders, we must recognize the divine mandate behind our jobs, companies, homes, and possessions. Our jobs are a mission field of people we can reach every day. Our schools are full of hurting hearts we can impact. Our communities are filled with individuals suffering from hopelessness and living with physical pain. And our homes are more than status symbols; they are platforms, positioning us in neighborhoods that need light, love and liberty.

But the questions remain, "Are we using the talents and positions God has given us to further His reach or are we merely looking for what pleases us?" The temptation to focus on selfish ambitions stifles God's purposes on earth and limits our fullest potential.

When we become selfishly consumed with our house, our bills, our bodies, our suffering and our needs, we lose sight of lost and hurting neighbors, co-workers and people around us who are crying out for help. But when we step out of our ivory white towers and allow God's Spirit to flow through us, we can indeed become catalysts of the change we want to see in the world.

MARKETPLACE PLATFORMS

"My workstation is my worship station. God calls us to the work we are doing. Therefore, He is interested in what we do and how we do it."
- Ken Costa, *God at Work*

In our lifetime, we will spend approximately 90,000 hours in the workplace. In those precious hours of our lives, no one is exempt from challenges, stress, and frustration that come with the struggle to find the winning edge, grind for power or merely provide for the family. Today, more than ever, we need God in the workplace, the marketplace, in schools and in our homes. We need men and women who say "YES" to become conduits of the Holy Spirit to a people starving for leadership worth following.

When my daughter turned 16, she was overjoyed to get her first job at Chick-fil-A. She launched into her new position, proudly wearing the required uniform and hat. It was like a badge of honor the first time she put it on. Then, after the first week of smelling like chicken and standing on her feet all day, she quickly realized that a job means hard work and applied effort, continual learning, emotional courage, and patience with the people she was called to serve. She woke up to the fact that life could be perfect if somehow people weren't involved.

People create pressures, often unrealistic expectations and frustrations to our ideal dream of peace and the pursuit of happiness. People cause our egos to roar and our own emotions to cry "foul". And yet, the very people who surround us at work and in life are our mission field in whom we have been sent to reach, love and impact with the love of God daily.

After that first week, Alexia came home ready to quit, asking, "Why do I have to do this job when it has nothing to do with my dream to sing and be a worship leader?" What she didn't understand was that her job was God's gift to her to effectively touch the world. Standing behind that counter, she was expressing worship to Him without ever singing a song. I told her, "Baby, those people that come into your Chick-fil-A are your mission field, and that cash register you stand behind is your pulpit. Worship God today by letting your light shine to everyone who walks up to your cash register. Be light. Be love. Be Jesus in the marketplace. And then, when you prove faithful to reflect Him in the little things, God can make you ruler over much." (Luke 16:10).

Perhaps you can understand those feelings of frustration with your job, career, employer or workplace. Ask yourself, "Why am I here? Why has LIFE placed me here, now, in this season? Have I done all I can do to be a conduit of light in the marketplace around me? Am I focused on scaling my numbers more than I am serving my co-workers? Do I reflect God and His love for humanity or am I a walking ego searching for personal recognition, affirmation, and significance through my efforts?"

If we merely live to fulfill our selfish motives of personal gain and notoriety, we are living for ego and will ultimately find it an empty path to suffering, broken relationships and defeat. However, when we recognize our true purpose and potential, we will see that every job, every negotiation, each challenge and every adversity we face is an opportunity to reflect God's love, power, and peace to the world around us.

MARKETPLACE MISSIONARY

I grew up in a Christian home as a preacher's kid. My grandfather was a pastor and missionary who founded a Bible College that equipped missionaries to be sent around the world. My dad followed in his footsteps and became a pastor and evangelist, but soon realized that paying the bills was tough when you were relying on the offerings of others. So, to help make ends meet, my dad jumped into sales and began going door-to-door selling perfume, soap, water filters and anything he could get his hands on to pay the bills. His ability to sell and build teams of other sales leaders soon led to great success which birthed a new dream in his heart. He longed to be an entrepreneur that used his profits to pay for his passion for ministry.

Though no one knew the name for it back then, my dad was a first-generation marketplace missionary, called to reach people right in the middle of their workday. He eventually became a successful real-estate broker, using his business as his pulpit and his profits as his way to fund his heart for ministry.

Consider this: We spend 40 to 50 hours a week at our jobs alone. We spend even more time in the marketplace shopping, going to school, attending sporting events and at entertainment venues. We live busy lives. Now, compare the time we spend in the marketplace to the average ONE hour a week we spend in a temple of worship or in a building where someone reads scripture to us or speaks a message, designed to grow our faith.

It's clear to see why Jesus established a new model of expansion in the marketplace. He knew the best way to reach hurting people would not be through the brick and mortar establishments made by man, but through the spiritual awakening of leaders, willing to GO and share their faith with others. That is why Jesus sent the Holy Spirit to live IN us and work through us.

1 Corinthians 6:19 - *"Do you not know that your bodies are temples of the Holy Spirit, who is in you, whom you have received from God?"*

That scripture doesn't say, "Your local church is the temple of God, and if you want to encounter Him, you must go there on Sunday." NO...it says, "YOU are the temple of God, and HIS Spirit is in YOU!" That changes everything. That means that God is counting on YOU to be the voice of hope. He wants YOU to lay hands on the sick. He wants YOU to bring freedom to those bound to addiction and oppression.

If your only act of church activity is sitting through a church service once or twice a week and serving as a greeter or usher, you are missing the mark. The term "going to church" has confused a lot of people. You don't "GO" to church. You ARE the Church and God is counting on you to take His presence to the people. You are the living, breathing Body of Christ. Now is the time to use your voice, your talents and your position in the marketplace to unleash the Holy Spirit around you.

The local assembly or "church" body you attend weekly should be a time of fellowship, testimony, celebration, worship, and a time to refuel and reflect on the week's accomplishments. It should be a collective time of sharing the good news of how you advanced the Kingdom of God at work or in your community. There should be stories of people who were healed, souls that were saved and ordinary people who are sharing the extraordinary message of Christ at their workplace, in their homes, and throughout their city. This is how the disciples and apostles expanded the church in the Book of Acts and how we should be doing it today in our jobs, homes and communities.

> **That is going to be the big SHIFT in today's spiritual communities. It's time to UNLEASH the body of Christ and teach them to get out of their seats and into the streets.**

Unfortunately, the "assembling together" that many know as church has all too often digressed into people comfortably sitting on Sundays, listening to a speaker talk about the Bible. As creative and inspiring as their messages might be, they don't scare the enemy. Satan loves seeing God's people pacified by motivational soliloquies that inspire listeners to simply "survive" another week at work or in life. But what scares the HELL out of the demons of darkness is when the Body of Christ recognizes the power within them to get up out of their seats and begin to take the power of God to the world around them.

Jesus poured out His Spirit on ALL FLESH, not just a chosen few. God wants to raise a massive army of believers to be deployed into world and BE the church. Be the light. Be Jesus in the marketplace. Be a revolutionary. This is the heartbeat of God.

PRACTICE WHAT YOU PREACH

Even as I write this, I am sitting in my office and can see my neighbor working in his yard. He is in his mid to late 70's, and He and his wife often sit on their front porch quietly enjoying their morning tea. Our relationship has been casual with "Good Morning" or "Hello". Otherwise, there has been very little conversation between us as they're not that talkative. Yesterday, however, my heart was moved with compassion for them as I observed the man putting a new flowerbed in his yard. I was busy, working on the final chapter of this book and I thought, "I wonder if I'll see him in heaven." For the rest of the day, I kept seeing him move about his yard but stayed focused on writing my book.

Again, the thought crossed my mind, "I wonder if his soul is right with God. Will he be gardening in heaven?" I have lived in this neighborhood for four years and I must admit that I have never had these thoughts, until now. As much as I felt concerned about his eternal peace, the voice of resistance continued saying, "You need to finish your book. You can talk to him later or maybe invite him to attend church service on Sunday."

Then, I realized, "How can I write a book, expecting other leaders to step out of their busy lifestyles and fulfill heaven's divine mandate upon their lives if I don't lay aside my important "to do" list and walk over to my neighbor and be Jesus at this moment?" So, I closed my computer and headed his way. As I approached him, I said, "Heyyyyyy Neighbor! Your yard sure looks great." He smiled and responded with a cordial "Thank you." I could hear Holy Spirit whisper, "Go for it, Staci! I have set you up for this moment."

I continued, "You know, I keep an eye on you every day as I sit in my office and I even pray for you as you work on your yard. Today, you were especially on my heart, and I was thinking, 'I wonder if I'll see him in heaven.' Do you believe in God?"

With a surprised look on his face, he said, "Well, yes, but we don't go to church."

My quick and bold reply was, "But do you believe in Jesus and have a personal relationship with Him?"

He said, "Yes, that is how we were raised. We just don't go to church anymore."

I replied, "Well, I suppose going to a church building doesn't make you a Christian any more than hanging out at a donut shop makes you a police officer."

He chuckled and responded, "That's right."

I continued, "I am glad to hear that I'll see you in heaven. Please let us know if we can ever serve you or your wife in the future. We would love to help in any way." I walked home feeling a great sense of peace as if the Holy Spirit was saying, "Well done, my good and faithful servant. Now go finish your book."

At that moment, my book was overshadowed by a much higher purpose: "Jesus said, 'Love your neighbor as yourself.'" (Mark 12:31)

Isn't it amazing how the enemy will try everything he can to keep us from getting out of our busy worlds and into the hearts of others? He sends distractions, busyness and mental opposition to blind us to the needs around us. His objective is to ensure our heads stay down with a "Do Not Disturb" sign on our little cubicle at work or even inside the four walls of our homes. He loves it when we think "going to church" fulfills our spiritual duty.

But God wants to UNLEASH His spiritual authority and boldness through us so that we can be equipped to be His agent of change at work, at home, throughout the marketplace, AND in our neighborhood. We are carriers of God's light, love, His message and His healing power to the world around us. Now is the time for a marketplace revolution of miracles to begin and it starts when we say "YES, God. Use me. Send Me. Flow through me and let my life, my job, and my talents bring hope, help and healing to the world around me."

For discussion or meditation:
What is your marketplace platform or mission field? Did you use your platform this week to reach the lost or pray for those in need?

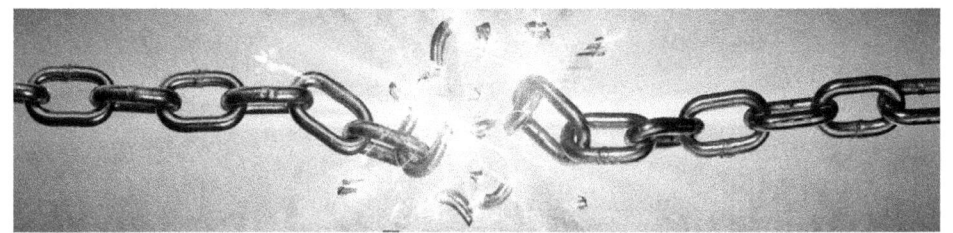

CHAPTER 2

ANOINTED FOR BUSINESS

Anoint (v): to smear or rub with oil or an oily substance

I grew up in the day and age when we suntanned our bodies by smearing on layers of baby oil or even worse -- Crisco. We rubbed it all over our bodies then laid on foil blankets, and then baked until we were "fried like chicken". Those were some crazy days, and unfortunately, no one stopped us. I don't suppose there was anything good about that season of ignorance other than it taught me what it means to be anointed and covered by something from head to toe.

To be "anointed for business" means that God empowers us with His Holy Spirit to do His work in the marketplace. He has lathered His greatness upon us and placed within us unique spiritual abilities that help us see, hear, and discern with a higher level of insight. You may not think that you have any special spiritual abilities, but you do! The events of your life have been a practice field for the spiritual gifts God will call you to use on behalf of His Kingdom. When I connected the dots of my past victories and failures, I began to realize that God had been preparing me for years to be anointed for business.

CONNECTING THE DOTS

When I was just a little girl, my after-school playground was my Granny and Papo's house. Attached to their modest home was the Bible college that they founded in Oklahoma, where they trained and equipped missionaries and sent them around the world. I loved going there because as soon as the staff and students would leave each day, I would run to the front offices and play in the reception area as if I was a big-time business owner. I pretended that customers were coming to my desk where I was making million-dollar transactions.

Those were the days when credit cards were swiped on a manual machine that held a 2-page carbon paper form and then the information of the customer was handwritten on the form. I loved hearing the swipe go across the raised letters and carbon paper. In my mind, I was making "big deal" transactions right there in the foyer of the Bible college, and I wouldn't stop until my mom called me for dinner and graciously invited me back to reality.

Those days of "big business" in the Bible college were a type of foreshadowing of the spiritual gifts of leadership, faith and prophecy that would become such an influential part of my marketplace ministry.

In addition to my young love for credit card swiping, I equally loved EVERYTHING competitive! Growing up, I was a bona fide tomboy who would rather be beating boys on the basketball court or playing tackle football after school. I eventually became an all-state basketball player and black-belt in mixed martial arts. I didn't know it then, but God was using those days of competition to give me a fierce boldness and a warrior-like DNA that would eventually position me both in business and ministry as a force of change for a generation in desperate need of liberation.

> Your life, no doubt, has been preparing you for something great.

If we peeled back your life like an onion, it would reveal God's sovereign hand upon your life. When I coach clients, this is a starting point as we help them connect the dots of their past with perfect 20/20 vision.

Looking back, you can begin to see why God has placed you in THAT job, in THAT city, as a father or mother to THAT child, as a husband to THAT wife, and why He had to use THOSE challenges to prepare you for such a time as this. YOU are powerful beyond words, and every obstacle or giant you have faced has prepared you to be anointed for business.

LICE AND INSECTS

The ancient origin of the word "anointing" came from the practice of shepherds in the field whose primary business activity was tending sheep, multiplying their flock and selling or trading them for eventual consumption. Sounds like a modern-day corporation of goods and services, right?

Stay with me. This part gets really good. In ancient days, sheep were a huge commodity and so was their meat, wool and skin. If a shepherd's herd of sheep were threatened, so was his job and his income, which is why protecting the herd was of great importance. Back then, the greatest threat to sheep losing their lives wasn't lions or bears or other predators. Instead, it was the lice and insects that would creep into their ears and kill the sheep from the inside out.

To combat this issue, the shepherds would anoint the sheep's heads with oil, a lot of oil. They would pour enough oil over the sheep's head that it would make the wool slippery and impossible for insects to get near their ears. That is also how the practice of anointing became symbolic of blessing, protection, and empowerment. The oil signified the Holy Spirit of God poured out on the head of individual people, consecrating or setting them apart for specific roles of leadership such as a king, prophet, builder, etc. (Psalm 133:2) In essence, they became the sheep of God, hearing God's voice and deflecting the voice of the enemy.

> Today, the enemy of your destiny knows that if he can attack your thoughts, your mind and become the predominant voice of your reasoning, he can kill, steal and destroy you from the inside out.

If the enemy can persuade you to disrespect your authorities at work, divide your loyalties in business, be a gossiper in the break-room, or subtly allow character flaws to creep into your environment, he can and will destroy your integrity over time. His highest ambition is to convince you that your time and energy should be focused on self-gratifying pursuits, personal power or worldly success. If he wins that battle, he owns your mind and distracts you from being the weapon of truth that God has destined you to be.

That is why, as you will soon learn, the Holy Spirit was sent to live in you and has anointed you for business in this generation. You are about to awaken to the irreplaceable value of the Holy Spirit's role in your life and how to protect your mind, heart, and body with the armor of God. By the end of this book, you will be educated, equipped and empowered with everything you need to take dominion in the marketplace and get back everything the enemy has ever stolen from you or your family. (Joel 2:25)

SLAYING GIANTS

David, the little shepherd boy who became famous for killing the giant, Goliath, was more than a kid tending sheep in a field. He was a young entrepreneur learning to rule and reign by overseeing the expanding inventory of his father's sheep business. The world saw him as the runt of the litter. The least among his brothers. The "other" child.

Perhaps the lies of the enemy have tried to make you feel less than significant as well. But when others saw a shepherd boy, GOD SAW A KING. David didn't have to rant and rave about his strength or importance. He didn't have to picket or protest for equality. He wasn't lured into taking selfies to try and convince the world he was someone special. Instead, in due season, God shifted kingdoms so that David's greatness could be seen.

David's primary job was that of a security guard. He guarded the herd of sheep against shoplifters like lions and bears while ensuring his dad's production line of sheep was healthy and on track. He also had to protect against the most prominent industry setback of his time which was caused by insects and lice. The strategy to protect against this #1 killer of production was to anoint his sheep with oil. But it was more than protecting his sheep that caused his success to surge. David equally had to protect his mind against the fear and insecurities of big business threats like the lions and bears that were on the prowl at night.

David had to stand in a position of mental strength and boldness every day at work despite opposition. When the time came for him to accept the part-time job as a food delivery boy, he ran to his brothers on the battlefield with food in tow. When he approached the front lines of battle that day, he was mentally, physically, and spiritually prepared to fight whatever threat came his way.

As he ran up to the front lines of the battle, he noticed the "elite" and highly trained soldiers of Israel had all retreated in fear because of the constant verbal insults of the Philistine, Goliath. But when young David sized up the situation, he recognized an entrepreneurial moment of financial opportunity. He asked, "What's in it for the man who kills that Philistine and gets rid of this ugly blot on Israel's honor? Who does he think he is, anyway, this uncircumcised Philistine, taunting the armies of the living God?" **(1 Samuel 17:26 MSG)**

Entrepreneur : *one who is willing to take business initiative, risking more than usual for financial opportunity.*

David saw a golden opportunity and had full confidence in the power of his God. He walked up to the negotiation field, ready to close the deal and gain the plunder. Perhaps he thought, "I've killed lions and bears in the middle of the night who were faster and more agile than Goliath, cloaked in his armor. And so, David used his weapon of choice, a slingshot. The battleground was his pulpit, and the gawking soldiers of Israel were his mission field. That day, he sent a prophetic message to the masses that His God was supreme in all things.

He was in the right place, at the right time, to become a future king worth following. The entire Bible is full of business examples of men, boys, women, and girls who yielded to a higher voice and greater calling than their surroundings. They learned to embrace risk and UNLEASH courage and boldness that we can learn from today.

Mary was a simple girl who said, "Yes." God was looking for a birthing ground for His Son and needed human participation to make the greatest miracle of all time a reality. When the angel appeared to Mary, she was a virgin and was pledged to be married to a man named Joseph. Saying "Yes" to God's request meant that she would be risking her life, her love, and her future dreams to take on the mandate of being a carrier of God's Holy Spirit and only begotten Son. It was reckless, unpredictable and unheard of for a virgin to be willing to be accused, rejected and scorned for something she didn't do.

God used a woman to birth the greatest revolution of all times, but before it could take place, Mary had to say, "YES." Today, Jesus, who grew up as a simple carpenter in the marketplace is now our Good Shepherd. He has been preparing you to be anointed to take His message to the streets with high confidence. Just like David, Mary, the disciples and the many women and men that stepped up to become the first wave of disciples in history, YOU were born for such a time as this. God is still using people to carry His message to the world today.

A CHURCH WITHOUT WALLS

Our generation has grown more and more cynical to religious ceremonies and Sunday services. People are craving a daily experience with God. Multitudes have left the four walls of the local church, temple or synagogue in pursuit of something more relevant to their everyday lives. Our generation is starving for the supernatural presence of God, but they are instead, filling themselves with mystical or paranormal counterfeits. Look at the entertainment industry: movies, games, and books about witchcraft, sorcery, wizards, and kingdoms of power pervade our homes.

Jesus faced this same challenge in His day, which is why He so boldly disrupted the religious system. He taught His disciples to step outside of the Sunday morning "come and hear" model, which seemed to have become corrupt, broken and ineffective in displaying God's power on earth. Instead, He gave his followers a bolder "go and tell" mandate that would move them into the marketplace, backed by signs and wonders to confirm His Word.

Today, less than 20% of Americans attend a local church assembly on a regular basis. Those who do go to church only spend ONE hour a week there on average. In many European countries, the percentages are even lower. According to Barna Research and the American Culture and Faith Institute, only 1 in 10 Americans have a biblical worldview, and just 4 percent of millennials believe the Bible is relevant for today. Some studies predict that by the year 2050 regular church attendance will drop to 11.7%.

The world has shifted its focus on who it listens to and now is the time to turn our efforts back to becoming the bold carriers of truth we were destined to be. That is the only way to stop the lice and insects of the enemy from penetrating the minds of our society.

We have a generation that listens more to fake media, bolstered ads and corporate hype than they listen to God. Of the 3.5 billion Google searches that occur every day, the top 100 searches don't even include a single search for God, religion, faith or anything biblical. When a nation no longer searches for God, you better believe God will send out laborers to search for His people. That is what a good shepherd does. When even one sheep goes astray, a good shepherd will leave the 99 other sheep to pursue the one. We must stop waiting for the sheep to graze into the local church. Now is the time to GO and find those who are lost.

That is why we can't expect our only reach to them to be our "come and hear" church services once a week. It is up to us to "go and tell" them about the good news in the halls of companies, schools, sporting events and at social venues that they frequent every day.

Jesus came to serve as an example of how to get out of our institutional comfort zones and penetrate the hearts and lives of people in the marketplace. He chose His sales team of disciples, not from the hierarchy of the synagogue, but from the ordinary migrants of the marketplace because they could speak the language of the people and could empathize and relate to their greatest needs. He reached hurting hearts right where they were. Jesus was a heretic that ate with tax collectors and sat with sinners and made it a point to mentor ordinary business leaders into becoming the cornerstone of His entire global network.

MARKETPLACE AWAKENING

In the early 19th century, the world was very dark, slavery was the norm, and people had grown cynical about the things of God much like they are today. But still, there was a remnant of men and women who hungered passionately for God. They were dedicated to pressing into the presence of God, praying for transformational change to sweep their generation. Soon, their hunger and thirst to be used by God birthed a powerful movement that paved the way for great reforms to take place, including the abolition of slavery.

I sincerely believe that we are entering a Marketplace Awakening that is poised to enlighten, empower and entrust marketplace leaders to be the catalyst for formidable change in our world. This Marketplace Awakening will yield a new generation of leaders who are filled with God's Spirit and who understand what it means to take dominion and authority over darkness and who begin to bring transformational change to the economy, society, and the Church at large.

Of course, when God is orchestrating a revolution of positive change, the enemy will do everything he can to distract us from God's ultimate plans and purposes. He will cause political upheavals through the search for power and shake a nation's focus with agendas of greed and ambition. He will use technology to hypnotize our attention away from time with the family and distract us from precious moments that could be utilized studying God's Word. His goal? To creep into our ears and our hearts, steal our attention, and destroy our peace.

For discussion or meditation: What are the loudest voices or greatest temptations that infiltrate your mind and try to steal your focus from being UNLEASHED as a leader worth following?

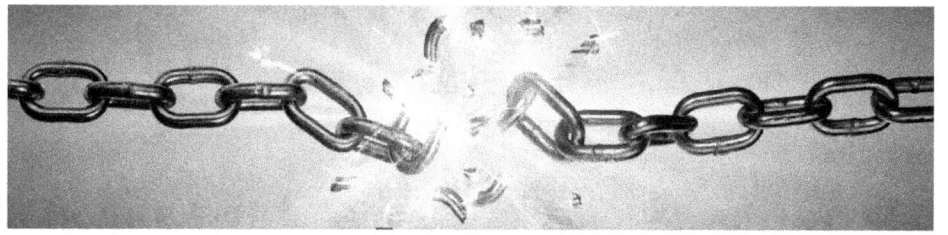

CHAPTER THREE

THE HUSTLE

As leaders and entrepreneurs, we've been taught how to hustle for profits, but all too often, we sacrifice peace in the process. Peace with profits is possible, but not without a transparent partnership with the Holy Spirit. To be UNLEASHED and Anointed for Business means that you take dominion as a leader in the marketplace and operate with unlimited potential, purpose, and power from the Holy Spirit. It means that you continue to perfect your skills, but you also surrender to be a conduit of God's will to use those skills within your community.

Today's leaders, influencers, innovators, and communicators must dig deeper than building companies, gaining followers, advancing technologies, and blending into cultural norms that lead to nothing more than human advancements. While these strategies grow profits, policies, and pocketbooks, they fail to feed the insatiable hunger of the human soul for spiritual peace and significance. Our evolution in technology has advanced while our development of spiritual maturity has stagnated or even digressed. Now is the time for a culture shift. It's time for heaven's culture or Kingdom to invade earth. (Matthew 6:10)

Culture (n): *the set of shared attitudes, values, goals, behaviors, and practices that characterizes an institution or organization.*

What you value most becomes the filter for your family, business or nation, which, in turn, creates the culture you embrace. Your values emit an aroma or ether that influences behaviors. A culture of spiritual apathy, for example, will yield spiritual starvation in its people. What you value most will be seen in the outcomes you produce. If you have a family that values prayer, you will create a richer spirituality than a family that doesn't. If you value kindness and compassion, you will see a culture emerge that emulates mercy and generosity in its people. If you value evangelism and healing, you will breed a culture of people that hunger to be used in those areas.

If we want to transform our company, community, family or nation, we must look at the culture of spirituality that we have embraced or rejected and why. In business, the power of culture can dictate productivity, performance, internal relationships, reputation, integrity and overall profits. Knowing how to create a healthy lifestyle in your family or office that breeds spiritual growth is even more critical that the products you sell, the people you hire, the home you live in or the money you produce.

In our current state of national crisis, division, hatred, racial tensions and in the many mass shootings across our nation, it is evident that when a nation turns from God, suffering ensues and an ether of hopelessness rests upon the people. A country, family or corporate culture that does NOT place a high value on spiritual maturity and development will eventually breed empty, selfish, divisive and power-hungry leaders who are never satisfied.

SOMETHING STINKS

As a kid, one of my favorite cartoon characters was Pepé Le Pew. He was the skunk that was always in search of love and approval. I remember watching Pepé on Saturday mornings and thinking, "Poor guy, he thinks he's so debonair, but no matter how hard he tries to portray himself as a perfect gentleman to the ladies, he still stinks." Unfortunately, we live in a "Pepé Le Pew" society that reeks of ego and perfectionism, but it never seems to be satisfied. We post selfies wanting the world to buy into our presumed lives of perfection and yet deep inside we reek of suffering and a lack of peace or satisfaction.

Our longing for success has given birth to a self-promoting "Me" generation that, much like Pepé Le Pew, is endlessly pursuing love in all the wrong places. The longing for more "likes," more followers and more attention has created an ether of attraction that locks so many in a prison of comparison. Think about it. You feel great about your home until you see the "Jones" family post about their new home and pool. Suddenly, your home seems inadequate, and you start longing for "more." Or perhaps, you are quite satisfied as a "single" man or woman until you see your friend snuggling with their fiancé and planning for their wedding. All of a sudden, you think, "When will it be my turn? Why do I have to be alone?"

While social media has been a tremendous asset to reaching beyond usual constraints of communication, its addictive power over our emotions and behaviors can be dangerous. It's like a drug that pulls us back in for more and distracts us from things that matter most.

I remember being at the top of my game in business with a network of over 250,000 sales leaders under my leadership and yet, because of my lack of "likes" or "followers" in social media, I felt like I was inadequate. Despite the blessings in my life, when I compared myself to other speakers, authors or business leaders, I felt inadequate. I thought, "If I feel this way, knowing I have a great marriage, a substantial income, God-fearing children, a wonderful home and a thriving ministry, imagine how this addiction for approval and comparison trap affects people around me who are still striving for success?"

Jesus and His generation faced similar temptations over 2,000 years ago. Humanity was self-absorbed, greedy, insecure, angry, and unforgiving. The disciples even compared themselves to each other -- wanting to be most "liked" by Christ. Even John wanted to be appreciated as he repeatedly described himself as John, "the disciple whom Jesus loved." (John 19:26) The "selfie" culture started way before our "selfie" generation hit social media.

> **When we place our pride before spiritual progress, we begin to smell like the dust of the earth instead of taking on the likeness of heaven.**

The culture of the earth is plagued with the disease of "ME" and fueled by egos searching for approval and acceptance. No one is exempt from gravity's pull towards an ether of selfishness. We've all sinned and fallen short of the mark of perfection. So, to give us access to a culture of grace and mercy, God sent heaven's culture to earth through His only begotten Son, Jesus.

Jesus was a living example of humility, love, kindness, generosity, sacrifice and ultimate servant leadership. (John 3:16) He left heaven's grandeur to come to earth and create a counter-culture to the selfishness that permeated humanity. When we take on the nature or character of Christ, that is when our enlightenment begins, and our most significant impact on the world is manifested.

Your life is a holding tank of what matters most to you. If you value love, you will bring love into the atmosphere around you. If you are an incubator of envy and strife, you will bring discord and division to your relationships and business. If you are full of joy and hope, you will brighten a room when you enter it, instead of it brightening when you leave.

YOU are powerful beyond words to either be an energy producer or energy reducer in your surroundings. At one point in my career, I had a cooking show and was featured on a morning talk show for moms. I used practical cooking examples of life circumstances to give leadership tips to our viewers. On one occasion, I used the example of making a wonderful homemade stew full of yummy goodness. My secret tip was: THE POWER OF A BAYLEAF.

There has been a long debate over the value of a simple dried bayleaf, but there is no denying that it makes the flavor uniquely better than a stew without it. While it's certainly not the essential part of a recipe like its companion, the vegetables or beef, a bay leaf holds significant power to change its atmosphere and bring out the more vibrant flavors of the other ingredients.

So, what's the point? YOU are a bay leaf, and your presence in a room may not seem significant. But you have the potential to shift the dynamics of your environment in a subtle, yet powerful way. A stew without bay leaves will not taste like it's missing something, yet there's no denying that when a leaf or two is included, something extraordinary happens. In the same way, you may not have the most impressive pedigree in the boardroom and perhaps others wouldn't even notice if you were missing. However, if you engage your spiritual potential, you can powerfully shift the atmosphere, emit a culture-shaking aroma, and bring out the greatness in others.

Whatever your vocation in life may be, you will have a choice in whether the room brightens when you enter or brightens when you leave. Will you emit an ether of humility, honesty, and integrity that raises the standard of biblical morality for the industry you represent, or will you follow the scent of the world, searching for approval and affirmation at all costs?

RAISING THE STANDARD

Will you be the gal at work that takes office supplies home in her bag thinking it's "no big deal"? Will you be the one who scrolls endlessly through your social feeds on company time? Will you be the actress that sacrifices her integrity to expand her public identity? Will you be the leader that stretches the truth and can only close a deal on the back of a white lie? Will you be the one that gossips in the breakroom about the boss's indiscretions?

You may not know it, but who you are, and what you represent makes a difference in how others see you. If you want to be respected and honored in the marketplace, you've got to raise the standard in your daily choices and overall integrity.

God wants to give you a heavenly aroma so that when others rub shoulders with you in the marketplace, they'll recognize and declare "That's a leader worth following!"

People may not attend church every day, but they will still be waking up every morning and heading off to work in the marketplace, shopping at malls, going to the gym, and congregating in social venues. And that, my friend, is where YOU enter the picture.

The sick and hurting people in the world will be more likely to experience God through YOU than they will a priest, pastor or evangelist. Why? If less than 20% of the world will even grace the steps of a church, where do you think the most excellent opportunity for revival is going to be today? Who is going to be the most influential voices of transformational change to a lost and hurting world? Do you think it will be from a minister they only see once a week at church or the men and women they associate with every day in the marketplace? YOU are the church. YOU are a living temple of the Holy Spirit.

1 Corinthians 6:19-20 TLB - *"Haven't you yet learned that your body is the home (temple) of the Holy Spirit that God gave you, and that He lives within you? Your own body does not belong to you. For God has bought you with a great price. So, use every part of your body to give glory back to God, because he owns it."*

God unleashed His power in the marketplace through Jesus, and that is precisely where He plans to UNLEASH YOU. NOW is the time to allow God to awaken you, position you and empower you to be His hands, feet, and voice to the world around you.

For discussion or meditation:
What areas of your life do you need greater humility? Are you willing to do anything for God?

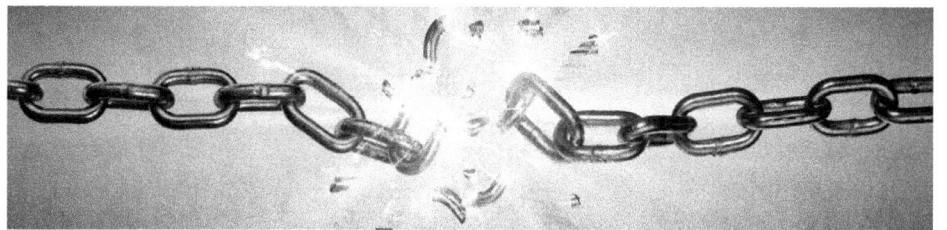

CHAPTER FOUR

DOMINION IN THE MARKETPLACE

In 2014, I was a Senior Executive for a telecommunications company based in Washington State. My position required my full attention as we scaled the company from scratch to $150 million in sales in less than three years. I was torn between my home in Frisco, Texas and my offices in Washington State. When I wasn't carrying out my corporate responsibilities, I was in my home office, producing training webinars, hosting international conference calls around the nation and being a homeschool mom to my two future world changers, Payton and Alexia. To say I was busy would have been an understatement. Society told me to hustle, get what you're worth as a woman, push your way to the top and win at all costs. I was exhausted, and my emotions were spent.

I didn't think I could add one more responsibility to my "plate" and then, one Sunday morning, our pastor announced they needed more singers for their worship team. On the one hand, I wanted to put my fingers in my ears and sing out loud "La la la" so I could ignore what I heard. And on the other hand, I knew I had been blessed with a God-given singing ability, and so I joined the team. Shortly after that, I had a dream that shook me to the core and awakened me to realize that God was about to unleash His power on earth.

In the dream, I was on stage, leading worship. The stage was filled with hundreds of light bulbs, salt shakers and a little lamb that was pacing back and forth as we sang our worship songs among a massive congregation and under high-tech lighting and sound. Everyone was caught up in the music and unshaken by the oddity of light bulbs and salt shakers on the stage. As the time of worship came to an end, I went to my seat in the second row, and the pastor stepped forward to give his message. The salt, light bulbs and lamb were still scattered all over the stage. As the pastor spoke about Jesus and salvation, the little lamb gently moved around him like a kitten looking for attention.

As I took my seat in the audience, I noticed that the base of the stage was sitting on top of a 5-foot platform. At the front of the bottom of the stage were bars and a padlock. All of a sudden, I could see a massive, roaring lion stalk over to the bars. Then I heard a voice in my dream say, *"Staci, the church has grown comfortable with the message of the Lamb, which is that of love, salvation, and grace. But I am about to UNLEASH the Lion of the Tribe of Judah on your generation in the form of signs and wonders, and they will know that I AM both the LION and THE LAMB. I am the source of all creation, the author of life and the great liberator of humanity. Prepare yourself for an outpouring of my Spirit with signs and wonders like have never been seen before."*

UNLEASH THE LION WITHIN

I woke up with such a sense of expectancy, knowing God was taking dominion and I hoped that I would have the privilege of being a part of such a revolution. I realized that the Lamb was the sacrificial representation of Jesus. The lightbulbs and salt were reflective of Matthew 5:13-14, "You are the salt of the earth." and "You are the light of the world." All three of those items represent the loving and forgiving elements of grace. But, more importantly, I believed that my dream signified a great outpouring of the power of God's glory that would be demonstrated through signs and wonders to this generation. God loves us just as we are, but He poured out the Holy Spirit because He loved us too much to leave us there. God wants us to grow beyond where we are into the powerful messengers we were created to be.

> **NOW is the time for you and I to recognize that God, the greatest of all innovators, and Jesus, the ultimate disrupter, are the same yesterday, today and forever.**

Jesus not only came as the spotless Lamb for our salvation, but He is also the Lion of the Tribe of Judah, giving us authority and power over the enemy today. His spirit IN us empowers us to take dominion over the things of this earth, including disease, oppression, depression, demonic spirits and forces of darkness.

We are called to be the hands and feet of Christ in the marketplace and a conduit of miracles to those suffering and in need. St. Teresa of Avila's words are incredibly applicable to this vision: "Christ has no body but yours, no hands, no feet on earth but yours. Yours are the eyes with which He looks with compassion on this world. Yours are the feet with which He walks about doing good. Yours are the hands, with which He blesses all the world. Yours are the hands. Yours are the feet. Yours are the eyes. You are His body. Christ has no body now but yours."

Get ready to take your place in this great awakening. The signs and wonders that are a part of all great revivals will not be confined to the four walls of a church or synagogue. No, they will come as they did in the days of the disciples, in the marketplace, through ordinary people who have extraordinary faith in a more than able God.

For discussion or meditation:
How can your life, your job, and your talents put you in a position to serve as the hands and feet of Christ?

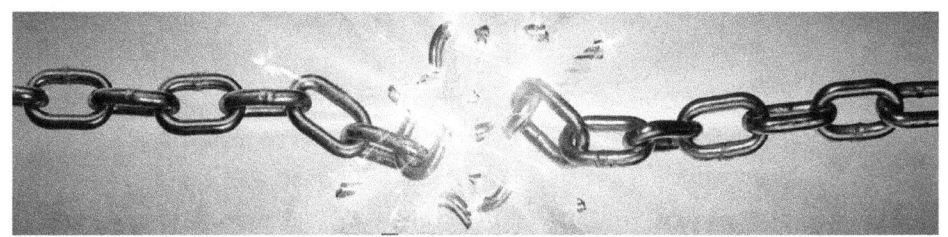

CHAPTER FIVE

KINGDOM PURPOSE

"Thy kingdom come, Thy will be done <u>on earth as it is in heaven</u>." – **Matthew 6:10**

Who am I? Why am I here? What is my purpose? These questions go hand in hand with a leader's relentless drive for progress and a sense of human accomplishment. We strive for new discoveries, improved technologies and intellectual advancements, searching for the WHY behind our primal existence. No matter how successful we become or how massive a kingdom we possess on earth, there is still an insatiable hunger for something more.

There are billions of dollars spent on Space research, and the Government has created a "Space Force" to protect us from impending wars in the sky. But there is an even greater war that is being waged in our souls, and its goal is to confuse our very purpose on earth.

I wrote a book entitled *Mission Possible* that was dedicated to helping people know that they are so much more than their title, talent or pedigree. It was my first book and my dear friend, renowned motivator, author and speaker, Zig Ziglar, wrote the foreword. He played an instrumental role in my life in that season, helping me understand the deeper WHY behind my vocal abilities and my talent to write. He challenged me to dig deeper into each chapter to help people see beyond the WHAT and into the WHY of life. He said, "Staci, there is so much more to life than what we do for a living."

When I fully understood what he was saying I realized that our careers or the platforms we stand on, would not transcend this life. We can't take them with us. But fulfilling our divine purpose will be what becomes the gateway to finding ultimate peace on earth. So, what is your purpose?

Your talent or job is NOT your purpose. They are merely platforms or mission fields that God will use you in to display His Kingdom on earth and to shine His light through you.

BORN TO REFLECT GOD

Ego wants power and attention. It strives for position. It tries to convince us that our purpose is somehow in our pursuits. But our ultimate objective is to point to the ultimate source of power -- God. It is not to boast of our greatness or search for man's approval through our job or achievements. That is ego's pursuit. Our highest purpose is to reflect God as a living, breathing, walking, talking, manifesting conduit of His healing power, salvation, and freedom to the world around us.

I was born in Dallas, Texas to very young parents (Mom was 17 and Dad was 18 when they married. They met when they were only 12 and 13). As young as they were, they had great faith. My grandfather was the pastor of a church in the South Oak Cliff community of Dallas. Dad played the piano at church and directed the choir and my mom played the organ.

When I was only eighteen months old, my parents faced the reality that I was a very sick little girl. After repeated bouts of pneumonia, and many tests, our family doctor diagnosed me with Cystic Fibrosis, a lung disease, that at that time, was incurable. Receiving such a devastating report would cause some people great fear and anxiety. But my parents had a clear revelation about God's power to heal, and they knew it was not a doctor or a diagnosis that had the final say in my destiny on earth. Instead, they believed that God was going to interrupt natural circumstances and perform a miracle for their little girl.

So, they did the only thing they knew to do. They prayed and called on other faith-filled leaders, pastors, and ministers to agree with them for that miracle. They spoke these words as if my life depended on them, "She will

live and not die, and she will proclaim the Good News of Christ to the nations." Immediately, the cough subsided, the lung congestion cleared up and the symptoms of Cystic Fibrosis were completely gone, and they never returned. From that day forward, I have never had another sign
of pneumonia, Cystic Fibrosis, asthma or any other dysfunction of my lungs. Isn't it amazing how the enemy tries to destroy us in the very place God intends to use us to impact the world?

Soon, the weakness that was diagnosed as lung disease was replaced with a powerful high-pitched squeal that my parents said was most obnoxious when my older brother would merely touch me or annoy me in some unforeseen way. But instead of letting the annoying screams frustrate them, my parents saw the annoyance as a miracle in progress. My vocal power and lung capacity eventually developed into a 5-½ octave singing voice that would open the doors for me to sing and speak on stages around the world with five U.S Presidents and declaring God as the miracle worker in my life. The same miracle working power that flowed through my body back then is equally available to heal today.

Hebrews 13:8 - *"Jesus Christ is the same yesterday, today and forever."*

God wants to demonstrate His power on earth by using us as conduits of miracles on earth. This is the beginning of Kingdom dynamics and the foundation of becoming *UNLEASHED and Anointed for Kingdom Business.*

This is the great mystery that so many people have forgotten or simply chosen to disregard. We are NOT the source of healing. Our talents are NOT the source of peace. Our jobs, titles or even family are NOT the sources of significance. Instead, it is the Holy Spirit that lives in us, as Christians, to empower us to do great exploits and reflect His glory to those around us.

We can spend our entire life striving for success but never find real and lasting significance. Why? Because we are so much more than the mass of flesh and abilities packaged in our earth suit or body. Life on this planet is God's gift to us. What we make of that gift is our gift back to Him. How we choose to surrender to His Spirit's leading will determine the value we receive from the time we have on this earth.

MARKETPLACE MISSION FIELD

John 14:12 NKJV - *"Most assuredly, I say to you, he who believes in Me, the works that I do he will do also; and greater works than these he will do, because I go to My Father. And whatever you ask in My name, that I will do, that the Father may be glorified in the Son. If you ask anything in My name, I will do it."*

Simply put....God wants to use YOU and flow His miracle-working power through you. The talents and passions that you were given are not about YOU! They are about HIM using you as a vessel so that HE will be glorified on earth. The sooner you let go of your insecurities and ego, and you allow God to use YOU, the sooner you will see His wonder-working power flowing through you. The marketplace around you is your mission field. Your job or talent is the platform you will use to communicate NEW LIFE to the world around you.

Matthew 5:14-16 MSG - *"You're here to be light, bringing out the God-colors in the world. God is not a secret to be kept. We're going public with this, as public as a city on a hill. If I make you light-bearers, you don't think I'm going to hide you under a bucket, do you? I'm putting you on a light stand. Now that I've put you there on a hilltop, on a light stand—shine!"*

God has a strategic plan for your life and talents. But those talents are NOT your purpose. They will not be the source of your happiness in life. Your talents and abilities may give you relevance or an open door to be in the marketplace, but they are not your purpose. They are merely an external expression of the higher purpose you were born to fulfill. As you read the pages of this book, you will discover that nothing can bring you more peace than knowing that you are tapped into your divine purpose and aligned with the source of all creation. As you find out the mystery of God's power that is living in you, and as you learn to recognize His voice, you will find that He will fill voids that no job, promotion, platform or relationship could ever be able to fill.

For discussion or meditation: How has God uniquely equipped or empowered you to impact people around you?

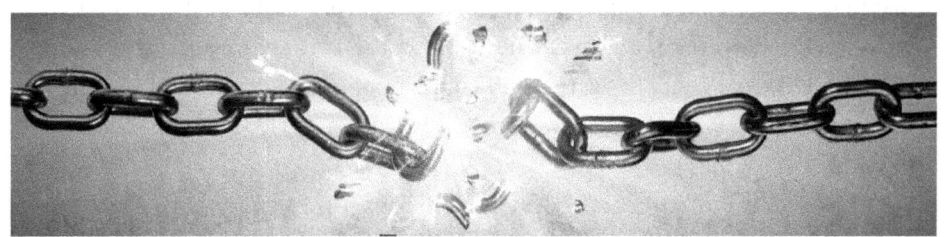

CHAPTER SIX

KINGS, PRIESTS & PROPHETS

I was just a child when I heard my father share a message about kings, priests and prophets and the roles they play in creating an eternal shift of consciousness in the human race. I could imagine being a queen of a mighty kingdom and I thought to myself, "If I were a queen, I would rule like Deborah, the judge who was willing to risk her life to lead an army into victory much like the courageous and bold heroine, Joan of Arc."

I also imagined being a wise prophet like Jeremiah, foreseeing into the future and becoming a spokesperson for God. I envisioned that someday, God would use my voice to bring a message of truth to nations.

And my understanding of the priesthood was reflected in how I would play church and kingdom rulership with my stuffed animals, lining them up as my royal subjects and Sunday School class. I offered them tea from my royal tea set and then I told them, "Jesus is the way, the truth, and the life!" The bunny was always the "hold-out," but with my prayers and great preaching, he finally gave in and repented. And when he did, I gave him a royal baptism in our kitchen sink.

Yes, growing up as a PK (preacher's kid) opened my mind to a world of possibilities and a perspective that most kids would never experience. I believed in my heart that God had an enormous plan for my future and that included being a prophet or spokesperson to nations.

I began to dream dreams and have extraordinary visions. And it wasn't just in the area of the things of God. I also believed I could be the first white girl signed to Motown, the first white girl on the Harlem Globetrotters and the first female President of the U.S. Dreaming was never an issue in my mind because I was taught that with God "anything is possible when you believe." (Mark 9:23)

I was blessed to be raised in a family who put a premium value on positivity and optimism. My parents ingrained in my brother and I that there was nothing we couldn't accomplish. They believed they were raising future world-changers, so they continued to encourage us to dream big, love unconditionally and seek desperately to be like Jesus.

In my young mind, not only did I see Him as a miracle-worker, but I saw Him as an unparalleled teacher, influencer and business man. He was a carpenter before He was ever noted as a miracle-worker or rabbi. As I grew older, I wanted to be like Him and that included a deep passion for being an entrepreneur and businesswoman.

At the age of 16, my dad gave me my first job as a receptionist in his business. I quickly became proficient in my communication skills and learned to use my bubbly personality and voice to brighten the day of anyone calling our office. My dad was my vocal coach and he made sure I practiced relentlessly. That practice and the stage presence I acquired from the many vocal competitions my parents entered me into, opened doors for me in the music industry.

By the time I turned 17, I was singing in Off-Broadway musicals, as well as singing with a 21-piece orchestra. At the age of 18, I was chosen to sing the Olympic Song, *Can You Feel It,* for the Opening and Closing Ceremonies of the Calgary Winter Olympics in Alberta, Canada. The world was opening its arms to my talents, and the marketplace seemed to be my stage.

When I returned from the Olympics, my greatest hope was to be signed with a Christian music label and fulfill the longing in my heart for ministry. Surprisingly, those doors never opened as it seemed my voice was more suitable for Motown than the local church.

Knowing I was still a little rough around the edges as a tomboy, my parents insisted on sending me to a modeling school to help me become more refined. The truth is, God was molding me into who I needed to be to fulfill His call upon my life. I often quote these words today: "You think you're waiting on God, but God is waiting for you to get ready." I needed preparation….and a lot of it!

Those few months of modeling, learning stage presence and working with top models in the city, equipped and empowered me to open my own modeling agency and fashion consulting business at the young age of 18 years old. It took off like wildfire and soon gave me an independent, financial lifestyle that put an end to any desire to attend a college or university.

Entrepreneurship was in my DNA, and I was embracing it wholeheartedly. Later that year, my dad taught me about residual income and so I added direct sales to my growing portfolio. By the age of 21, I had become the youngest National Marketing Director and member of the President's Advisory Council of a billion-dollar water and air filter company.

See a pattern? I was a go-getter, a visionary and a dreamer with a natural gift for the marketplace. God was using my competitive nature to help me drive business while teaching me valuable skills in communication, negotiation and contractual wisdom. Tradition wisdom said, "She has a kingly (business) anointing" which was true; however, I learned early in life that making money never seemed to bring me true fulfillment. I craved so much more than what money can buy. The priest in me was longing to be unleashed as well.

CHRIST IN YOU

Despite my business success, I was never more fulfilled than when I was using my ministry gifts to teach, sing and pray for those in need. I knew I had to hold firm to my business responsibilities, but I also desired to be a mouthpiece for God and use my voice to bring hope, help and healing to my generation. It was an internal battle of emotions because culture told me that I needed to choose one or the other: king or priest, businesswoman or full-time ministry. The world placed such high value on business success and financial gain that I continued to hunger for the world's approval.

I had read in Colossians 1:27 that Christ lives in us so I continued to battle with the thought, "Why would God want us to choose between king OR priest? Doesn't it seem probable that since Christ lives in us, that His nature of king, priest, and prophet lives in us as well?" Are we not called to emulate Christ on earth? He is the same yesterday, today and forever and it seems that his divine nature would also be alive in me, as well.

Paul said in 1 Corinthians 11:1: "Be imitators of me, just as I also am of Christ." And so, I chose to live outside of the norm and believe that God could use my life in the marketplace, while simultaneously using me to be His spokeswoman of hope to those I reach.

He is still King, Priest and Prophet and His miracle-working power will be most recognized in the marketplace through ordinary people like you and me who are fulfilling our role in the same way. Sure, we may operate more powerfully in specific areas than others, but if Christ lives in us, then we should dig deep to learn the wisdom of the FULLNESS of all that His Spirit provides to us.

For discussion or meditation: Do you operate more as a king, priest or prophet in the marketplace?

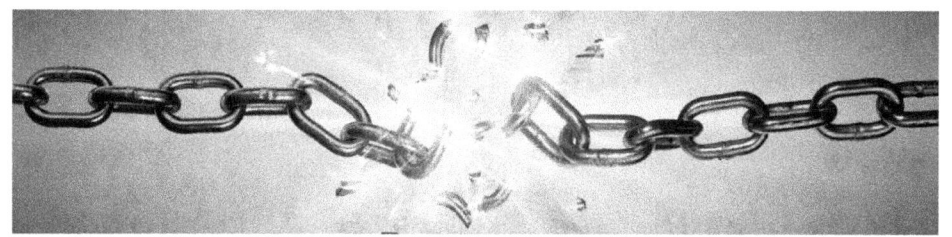

CHAPTER SEVEN

KINGDOM MENTALITY

KINGDOM (n): *a realm in which a king or queen has sovereign authority; a king's domain or territory of government where the people reflect its culture.*

THE KINGDOM OF GOD = *the territory of God's rule and reign on Earth, where His government is sovereign, and His authority can not be challenged.*

As God-fearing kings (or queens) in this modern world, we are to be positioned in seats of authority that give us opportunity to rule and reign on behalf of the Kingdom of God in our jobs, businesses, homes, and communities. Effectiveness in the marketplace is not a reserved privilege for a few positional leaders. Instead, being effective in our jobs, grocery stores and restaurants is the way God makes His presence and His Kingdom known. Almost everyone will work in the marketplace in some capacity in their lifetime. Currently, 71% of women with children under the age of 18 have at least one, sometimes two jobs. We spend a vast majority of our awake time working normal jobs and interacting with normal people.

To be a king in God's Kingdom means that are positioned under the leadership of THE KING, Jesus, who presides over all earthly kings in the marketplace. (1 Timothy 6:15) As His followers, we have been given dominion to rule and reign under His authority on earth in the marketplace and within our homes.

Jesus, THE KING of kings, is seated at the right hand of God the Father. When we embrace our royalty or citizenship in His Kingdom, we posture ourselves as kings under His rulership and become His Body or ambassdors on earth. He is our head. We are His physical representatives in this world. (Ephesians 1:20-23)

PRIEST (n) – *an authorized minister or elder dedicated to performing the sacred rites of a religion on behalf of the people, often standing as a mediator between man and God.*

Before Jesus, who ultimately became the official High Priest, people looked to elders in the church, often called bishops, presbyters, pastors or priests to perform this role and other priestly duties. Traditionally, one had to be chosen, ordained or of a particular office to perform such spiritual rites for the people. Those hierarchal leaders were often elevated to a position that enabled them to perform specific duties for the people and carry out special responsibilities as a mediator between the people and God. The people, in turn, came to the temple or synagogue to listen to the priest and be forgiven of their sins. It was the ultimate "come and listen" pattern of priestly ministry.

1 Peter 2:9 (NKJV) - *"But you are a chosen generation, a royal priesthood, a holy nation, His own special people, that you may proclaim the praises of Him who called you out of darkness into His marvelous light."*

Jesus came and sent the Holy Spirit to disrupt that model. Instead of the ministry being confined to a building, priest or pastor, God unleashed His Spirit to live inside of us and anyone who chose to believe. He shifted the plan from being confined to a "few good men" in leadership, into turning housewives, doctors, fishermen, children, harlots, tax collectors and ordinary people like you and me into extraordinary carriers of His Spirit on earth.

Jesus taught us how to be a part of His Kingdom of priests that individually hear God's voice, know His way, teach His truths, and heal the sick. That makes you both a king and a priest in this world.

Revelation 1:6 (NLT) *says, "He has made us a Kingdom of priests for God his Father. All glory and power to him forever and ever! Amen."*

As priests in the marketplace, we have been set apart for the purpose of teaching others what being a Christ follower looks and acts like. We, much like the priests of old and Jesus Himself, should be set apart as a counter-culture to the world around us. When others look at us, they should see a reflection of God's Word and know us by our unique love and consistency.

Our times of gathering together for worship services should be a designated time to get refueled for the week and be encouraged by the unity of God's people to get back into the marketplace as the hands and feet of Jesus. Sunday services or community gatherings should be a time of hearing the testimonies of others while getting equiipped on how to better mobilize our gifts in the marketplace.

Unfortunatley, many churches are more of a motivational session that puts attention on a speaker or small handful of talented musicians instead of focusing on equipping the people for another week of Kingdom business in the marketplace. You and I are a part of that Kingdom of priests, and God wants to use our lives to reflect His goodness and mercy to the world around us each day.

PROPHET (n) – *an effective or leading spokesman for a cause, doctrine, or group, especially one who is regarded as an inspired teacher or proclaimer of the will of God.*

Paul made it very clear that, not only are we kings and priests, but we are also called to be prophets or spokespeople of God's divine wisdom. (1 Corinthians 14:5) As prophets for God, we must take time to pray, listen and perceive what God is asking us to share with the people we are called to influence. If you have a family, company, team, or an organization that looks to you for leadership, then your ability to cast vision as a marketplace prophet will be critical to your success and theirs.

The prophet admonishes, warns, directs, encourages, intercedes, teaches, counsels and brings the Word of God to the people and calls the people to respond. As leaders in the marketplace, we need to grow in these areas to be truly effective in our places of business.

Ezekiel was a prophet in the Old Testament that not only spoke God's will, but he was called by God to be a watchman over God's Kingdom. Jesus and John the Baptist were prophets. The disciples were called to be prophets. Their responsibility was to look out for the people, discern potential harm, and tell the people how to make needed course corrections in their lives.

Ezekiel 33:1-11 (MSG) - *"Son of man, speak to your people…You, son of man, are the watchman. I've made you a watchman for Israel. The minute you hear a message from me, warn them."*

Most leaders have never considered themselves prophets or evangelists to their staff, family or followers. But Jesus gave us the most significant examples of how to do this in the marketplace, in our churches and to our closest friends and family. We are watchmen or seers who are responsible for casting a clear and compelling vision that lead others to action.

ESTABLISHING KINGDOM ORDER

We, like Jesus, are called to build God's Kingdom on earth. It is our responsibility to do our part as kings who create provision, as priests who seek intimacy with God, and as prophets who pray for wisdom to know His will and help the world to understand His purposes. Not only is this a powerful Kingdom strategy, but it is also a wise business model that places us in a position of strength and certainty.

When we take on a Kingdom mindset, we will grow more and more passionate about our role in the marketplace. We should be helping care for the needs of the people while also providing spiritual wisdom for them to follow. Paul, the apostle, was a very educated scholar and tent-maker who used his business in the marketplace as a platform for his ministry.

Ask God how He plans to UNLEASH you in the marketplace. Soon, you too will see that the Holy Spirit has empowered YOU to do what Jesus did, and even more for your generation.

For discussion or meditation: What do you respect most about Jesus' style of leadership?

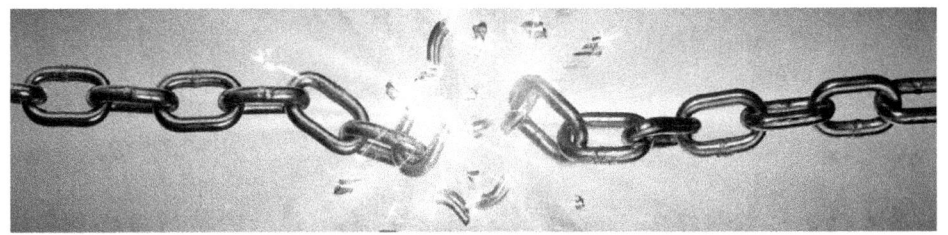

CHAPTER EIGHT

CEO MINDSET

In today's fast-paced world of rapidly expanding technologies, highly competitive workplaces and volatile economic conditions, people are continually searching for ways to stay relevant in their trade so that they can increase their worth or value in the marketplace. How does a young administrative assistant become indispensable? What can you do to rise to the top of your game? Is there a creative way to gain an edge in your work environment and be noticed as a remarkable asset to those around you?

Whether it's the value you bring to your company or family, having the right mindset is critical to maximizing your full potential. When personal performance begins to lag, or organizational ineffectiveness sets in, it's time to ensure that we are operating with a Kingdom mentality and a CEO Mindset. That includes taking personal initiative to treat our personal and corporate surroundings as if they were being viewed by the BOSS daily. When we have a Kingdom mentality, we treat the people, places, and things around us with a sense of ownership and respect.

You and I are the CEOs (Chief Executive Officer) of our lives. I've heard people refer to God as their CEO, meaning that they want Him in charge of their business. But, from a practical business perspective, I find that to be a misinterpretation of the actual role of the title. The role of CEO is all about making tough decisions and delegating responsibilities to well-equipped leaders. God does not make decisions for us. YOU and I are responsible for being decision makers, giving clear direction, and setting plans in place for our work, family and life. God might be our highest influencer, advisor, or Chairman in making those decisions, but ultimately there must be a CEO present, on earth, to take responsibility for the outcomes of the organization.

In 2009, I was hired as an executive consultant to help shift the culture and future of a struggling health and fitness company. The company had grown stagnant and financially insolvent. Despite the weak state of the company's financials, they still had thousands of happy and satisfied customers, and hundreds of passionate sales associates dedicated to doing whatever was necessary to turn the company around. The CEO and President had been leading the charge for 22 years, since its inception.

After an in-depth audit and analysis of the company, it was clear that they didn't have a product or people issue. Instead, they had a leadership issue. The CEO failed to make critical, necessary decisions about the brand and its financial condition and therefore, he had lost the faith of the people both internally as well as in his external sales leaders.

The more he and I worked on a plan to reinvent the company, its brand and its culture, the more we realized that a difficult decision needed to be made on behalf of the future of the company. He needed someone to step in alongside his leadership, regain the heartbeat of the people, and rebrand the company as a fresh and current leader in the industry. That meant he needed to step aside to allow someone else with a new perspective to intervene and lead for a season.

I was hired as the one to step in as his partner as Senior Vice President. I was immediately thrust into a whirlwind of corporate responsibilities. The most painful of my duties was making tough decisions about who would keep their jobs and who needed to be dismissed. It certainly wasn't my nature to terminate anyone, but in order to provide the financial relief the company needed, I had to make the tough decisions that were absolutely necessary.

My emotions were all over the place each time I had to meet with someone to give them the news of their termination. My secret sauce to gaining the emotional fortitude I needed was to call my mom for immediate prayers and moral support. Her spiritual alignment helped me "get a grip", dry my eyes and emerge as the empowered leader I needed to be in the moment.

When I accepted my position, I opted to take an old storage room as my new office. This allowed me to take something old and give it new life, new paint and a new purpose. It was also what we were doing with the company. I painted the walls of the large storage room a bright red and fancied it up with a modern look and feel, large glass windows and an open door policy.

I made sure the atmosphere was inviting and fresh, but also fiery hot to signify my passion for new beginnings and a relentless work ethic. To add fun to the bold message I was sending, I made sure to always have an abundant supply of Hot Tamale© candies available for anyone that passed by.

This sent a two-fold message. The first was that it was an open invitation to partake in sweetness that stemmed from my office. Second, it was a clear message that I was here to do business and bring the heat, if necessary. No doubt, some loved me, some feared me, some didn't like me, but once the cleaning was done, they all appreciated me for my bulldog tenacity and efforts.

As we shifted the attention off the President's leadership, I showed and conveyed fierce love for the company's culture and values, and soon, the sales leaders believed a corporate savior had arrived. I wasn't shy or silent about my faith, so they knew that God was up to something major. Literally, resurrection come to the company.

During the first six months, many necessary changes were made to implement a God-centered company that would become a source of hope, help, and healing for others. Employees and the sales field soon had hope for a new future. Together, we turned a product manufacturer into a company that was genuinely focused on creating transformational change in the lives of its customers and throughout the marketplace.

We redesigned the brand, terminated stagnant internal leaders and developed a social strategy that included a powerful stewardship campaign that shared profits and warehousing with local non-profit companies. We also redesigned their compensation model to give back to the people in an honest and integrous way.

I was humbled that God used me in such a powerful way to help that company make a monumental shift that caused it to continue to be thriving today. The real applause goes to the CEO and President for recognizing a need for change and making some tough decisions to turn the company around. Great leaders give up their right to be right, and instead, they do the right thing so that the right outcomes can take place.

God wants us to have a CEO mindset no matter what our title or position might be. That means that we see the company we work for from an owner's perspective. When we have a CEO mindset, we humble ourselves as servant leaders and become willing to do WHATEVER is necessary to make our company and our team successful.

SERVANT LEADERSHIP

Great leadership is not determined by our title but by our ability to influence the atmosphere around us. We might be a receptionist at the front desk of a company or the janitor mopping the floor, but we are still able to make sound decisions that impact our corporate culture and cause positive outcomes to take place.

CEO and Founder of DOSH, Ryan Wuerch, described this mindset to a think tank of leaders at the University of Washington. He said, "*The CEO Mentality*™ is not a title, but rather the ownership mindset an individual has in life. Becoming and being a CEO isn't just a matter of chance, family fortune, politics or personality. Rather, it is the result of consciously developing the core competencies and key attributes of leadership coupled with a mindset of success."

This quote and the teaching around this mindset had a profound impact on my leadership and how I trained the staff to take ownership of that company. As a part of our transitional process, I met with the staff and explained why every job is significant in shifting the culture. "A CEO Mindset," I said, "is about influence, responsibility, and impact." I looked at the front desk receptionist and asked her if she thought she could have a "CEO Mindset"?

She looked at me, confused. I explained it to her like this; "You are the first face people see when they walk in the front door. Your voice is the voice they hear when they call. How you come across to the outside world speaks volumes about the character, culture and compassion for our company's brand."

I went on to recommend; "The next time a shipment is dropped off by the UPS guy, ask him how his day is going. Ask him if you can get him water or soda and find out what his favorite drink of choice might be. The next time you see his truck pull up and he comes into the office, have that same drink waiting for him so you don't have to ask. It will say to him that you and the company care about him. His life makes a difference, and his happiness is our pleasure.

Make decisions that make a difference. That is what it means to have a CEO mindset. Eventually, you will have that UPS guy talking about your company at the bar, at church or wherever he frequents. Why? Because you decided to LEAD. You, as the receptionist, stepped out of an employee mentality into the CEO mindset of influencing change."

An exceptional CEO is not one who wields power over others, but he or she is the greatest servant of the vision, willing to do WHATEVER is necessary to carry the vision to scale. Great CEOs treat every area of the vision or business as if it was the most essential piece to the puzzle. With such power also comes great responsibility to delegate authority, make wise decisions and empower others to get the most excellent job done. That is the strength of true leadership. Great leaders SERVE the vision, not the outcome or the applause.

AN OWNERSHIP MENTALITY

When we take on a CEO mindset of the company we work for, we are treating the business like it's our own. When we have a CEO mindset about God's business, we will treat His Kingdom as if it were our own and serve it with our life. Scripture tells us to do ALL that we do as if we were working for Jesus Himself.

Colossians 3:23 - *"Whatever you do, work at it with all your heart, as working for the Lord, and not for man."*

The way this scripture is expressed is how we should see our jobs and our workplaces. How we view our job and workplace determines its meaning and purpose in our life. That's why it's so important to see our jobs from a heavenly perspective.

Now you might say, "But, Staci, you don't know my boss and co-workers. They are annoying, irritating and even corrupt!" But God knows what it will take to influence your boss and impact your company with the love of Christ. God, very well, may have selected you to be His ambassador in your workplace. Is it not the sick that need a doctor?

Mark 2:17 – *"On hearing this, Jesus said to them, "It is not the healthy who need a doctor, but the sick. I have not come to call the righteous, but sinners.""*

So, until He directs you to move, BE JESUS in the darkness of your surroundings and be light in your workplace. No job is too menial, and no person in it is too insignificant for God to reach. He wants us to take Him to the offices, prisons, schoolhouses and even crack-houses of the world.

"Leadership is influence. It's nothing more and nothing less." – John C. Maxwell Having a CEO mindset means that you shift rooms like a thermostat. A thermostat changes the room, but a thermometer only reflects it. So, if you are in a break-room and everyone seems to be moaning or complaining about their job or this or that, don't follow suit. Instead, sprinkle your pixie dust of God's love and positivity in the room and make shift happen. That is your role in your family and the marketplace. You are called to influence the world around you and reflect the Holy Spirit within you.

Isn't that what Jesus did as our example? He wasn't looking to "be the man." He was seeking to empower man to run His Kingdom. He doesn't push us into submission. Instead, He leads by example.

For discussion or meditation:
How can you have a better CEO Mindset at work or home?

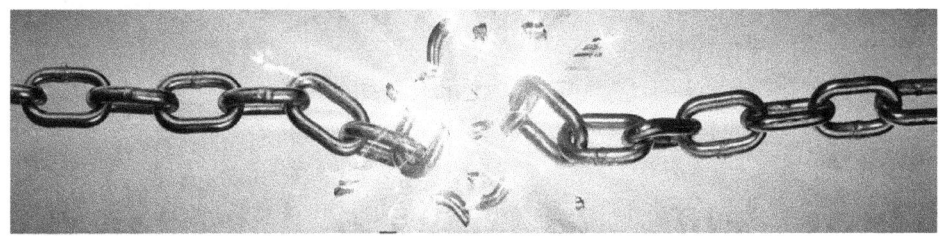

CHAPTER NINE

MARKETPLACE REVIVAL

"Being a Christian is more than just an instantaneous conversion - it is a daily process whereby you grow to be more and more like Christ." – Rev. Billy Graham

On February 20, 2018, I came out of REM sleep into that place where you are neither asleep or awake but somewhere in between. As I laid in my bed, I had a vision in living color. In it, I saw a massive tent spread over four pillars in the marketplace. It looked like a giant revival tent, and yet the center of the tent was not lifted up, so it sagged in the middle, preventing people from passing through safely.

Then, I saw massive cross beams floated in under the tent to lift the fabric high into the air. As the tent was complete, I heard a voice in the vision say, "Now is the time for marketplace revival. I have spread my covering over the marketplace, and I have called you and a hidden remnant of others who have prayed and hungered for revival, miracles and signs and wonders. I will use the marketplace to draw all men to me."

It was such an encouraging vision, and I shared it with my husband, believing that God was about to do something remarkable in and through us and our businesses. Little did I know that the very next morning, on February 21, 2018, one of the most celebrated revivalists of all time, Rev. Billy Graham, would pass away and graduate to his eternal home in heaven.

Chills rushed through my body as I considered the magnitude of my vision the night before, and what it could mean to this generation. Until that day, I had NEVER had a vision or dream about tents over the marketplace, and yet, the very next day, a patriarch of tent revivals had been elevated to His eternal reward. Coincidence? I don't think so!

I was blessed to be raised in a "revival" ministry where the power of God, as well as the salvation message, was fully alive. My father and grandfather were a part of many notable healings and miracles in those tent revivals, and it allowed me to see, firsthand, the healing power of Christ today.

THE LION AND THE LAMB

While I feel genuinely called to the message of the Lamb, which is the message of salvation, I also see that we are now experiencing an outpouring of the Holy Spirit in the form of signs and wonders in the marketplace like never before. This outpouring is the work of the Lion, which is God's miracle-working power.

As I meditated on the Lion and the Lamb, I suddenly realized, that the Lion in my earlier vision represented God's justice, power, authority, miracles, deliverance, dominion and courage to stand boldly in the face of adversity. God was not only concerned about our salvation and the work of the Lamb, but He was passionate about our healing, restoration, and deliverance, too. But such a balanced revival of salvation AND miracles would, no doubt, come with a price to those who choose to carry it to the marketplace.

Indeed, this was true of Christ, the apostles, and the early church. They were beaten, stoned and ultimately crucified. They were criticized, ostracized and ridiculed for their radical faith in God's power and bold desire to see His healing virtue sweep the nations and point back to the omnipotence of God. They disrupted the status-quo and were willing to boldly proclaim the Gospel in the marketplace.

As I was writing this book, I was reminded of how God "nudged" me to "practice what I preach" when it comes to being a radical voice in the marketplace, even in uncomfortable situations. I was on the tennis court, playing in a foursome, when I thought, "I wonder if these ladies know God."

I had been playing with this same group of powerhouse women for a year and had always been very vocal about my faith, my family, and church but had never asked them about their beliefs. So, when the thought crossed my mind, "Do they know Jesus?", I knew that God was asking me to step out of the tennis match and connect with their hearts.

We completed a set when I asked, "So ladies, will I see you in heaven? Will we get to play tennis together like this forever?"

They just smiled so I continued, "Do you believe in Jesus as the Son of God? I mean, are you and I still going to be tennis partners in heaven?"

An awkward pause followed the uncomfortable moment until they giggled and said, "Well, yes we will!" It was a moment of testing…not for them, but for me. Was I willing to stop what I was doing and obey the voice of God, even when it felt uncomfortable?

Later, during another set, one of the gals stopped play and said, "So, you've got me very emotional today with all this spiritual talk, and I've been thinking about something. I have been having pain in my back that hasn't seemed to go away."

Taking that as an open door, I said, "Well, let's pray right now. God loves you and wants you healed." So, together, with the other ladies, we stopped on the court and prayed. God has continued to take our tennis matches deeper and deeper each week as we now, openly, discuss miracles, faith, and evangelism together. That is what it means to BE the church in the marketplace and to use our tennis courts, cash registers, and offices as the pulpits and platforms to evangelize this generation.

Far too long we have been a people GOING to church but avoiding the responsibility of BEING the church in the lives of those who need Him most. Jesus showed us a better way by teaching us to go to the sick and hurting, and extend God's love to them, no matter who they are or what they may or may not believe. (Mark 2:16-17)

GOD IS UP TO SOMETHING GOOD

God unleashed His power in the marketplace through Jesus, and that is precisely where He plans to UNLEASH YOU. NOW is the time to allow God to awaken you, position you and empower you to be His hands, feet, and voice to the world around you.

God is doing a new thing. (Isaiah 43:19) He is unleashing the fullness of His Spirit on this generation. Marketplace revival will not be limited to one or two leaders but it will come through the lives of THOUSANDS of hungry God chasers who say "Yes, Lord, use me!"

Acts 1:8 (TLB) - *"But when the Holy Spirit has come upon you, you will receive power to testify about me with great effect, to the people in Jerusalem, throughout Judea, in Samaria, and to the ends of the earth, about my death and resurrection."*

God wants to reach the lost through you. God wants to do miracles through YOU. Why? Because He wants this generation to see that His power is higher than the human-made idols of worship that our society continues to revere. God is a jealous God that will not share His glory with Hollywood, Washington D.C., Silicon Valley or any other hub of human-made power. God wants all eyes on Him, and He will use mere humans to be the conduit of miracles if they will give Him the glory. That is the same reason why Jesus performed miracles. To point toward the Father and cause the lost to run to Him in total surrender.

Now is the time, this is the place, and YOU are the one that God wants to birth revival through in the marketplace around you. Your life, your talents, your job and your family are all bestowed upon you as gifts from the Father to empower you to connect with the world around you. Your purpose is not to be seen or known, but to make God known, and for the Lion and the Lamb to be known through you with an unprecedented impact on the earth.

For discussion or meditation:
What area of the marketplace do you have a burden for that God needs to impact with His light?

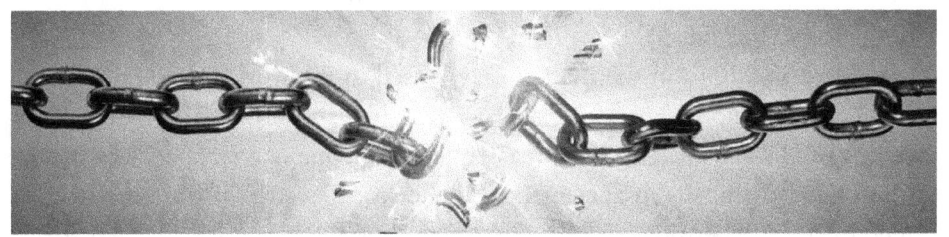

CHAPTER TEN

MARKETPLACE MAVERICKS

MAVERICK (n): *an unorthodox or independent thinker: one who lives "outside the box" of conformity*

The greatest innovators and thought leaders of our time are launching unconventional ideas and groundbreaking strategies that are changing society. We recognize maverick leaders because of their incredibly creative, innovative and original thinking. We revere them because of their ability to take massive risks that disrupt the status quo and shift global consciousness to a new place of greater effectiveness. Some of today's modern mavericks in business include the late Steve Jobs, Sir Richard Branson, Oprah Winfrey, Mark Cuban and Elon Musk.

The power of maverick leadership is that it shakes things up and sees the world as it should be, not merely how it is. It paves the way for future generations to live outside of the norms of current limitations and brings hope for a new day. Maverick leadership cuts through mountains to create highways for future generations.

Jesus was the greatest maverick of all time. He was unorthodox, unparalleled and unquestionably independent in His ability to live outside of cultural norms. He was all man, yet He was God in the flesh. He was compassion personified; however, He had all power over the things of this world. He was genius with great humility. He was heaven wrapped in humanity so that we could experience a supreme example of how to take dominion in this life.

Jesus was born in the marketplace, raised in the workforce, and spent His entire public life breaking social norms. In those days, the cave-like setting of His birth was a lower area of a family's living quarters – a place that often housed animals in ancient Israel. The word "stable" is used because, much like a modern-day gas station, it was where they refueled or fed the donkeys that were used for transportation. (Luke 2:7)

Why is that so important know? You would think the King of Kings would have required his entrance to the planet earth in a royal palace or holy tabernacle of worship, but not this King. He was a maverick and an out-of-the-box leader who came with a message of hope that would transcend human-made kingdoms and synagogues. It was God's plan to come to earth through Jesus, wrapped in human flesh as an ordinary man, so that He would understand, feel and experience every detail of the human life. He was the humble son of a carpenter and soon became an apprentice and young entrepreneur in His father's business. Jesus was raised in the workforce, knew the struggle of man, and yet spent His entire public life breaking social norms.

Perhaps that is also why He chose most of His followers from the marketplace:. They were full-time business owners, fishermen, tax collectors, doctors, and everyday entrepreneurs with a passion for using their life for something great. Jesus wanted marketplace leaders who would use marketplace venues to spread His message to the masses.

Even after the Holy Spirit was poured out as described in the Book of Acts, the disciples didn't confine their message to synagogues or spend their resources on opulent temples. They didn't look for extravagant places of worship but instead, moved throughout the streets and into the homes of the people daily. This is a model that would greatly benefit the Church today. Low overhead…high impact.

Today, we spend millions of dollars on state-of-the-art sound systems and epicenters of worship, hoping to attract the masses into buildings where the message of Christ is preached. But Jesus, followed a very different model. His miracles and His love were the drawing card of the New Testament. The greatest expansion of the Church today will take place when God's people, who ARE the temple of the Holy Spirit, go into the marketplace with the full power of His presence in operation. This was how the disciples lived.

Acts 5:42 - *"And every day, in the temple and from house to house, they did not cease teaching and preaching Jesus as the Christ (the anointed one and His anointing)."*

Jesus' grew up learning his trade in the marketplace as an apprentice in his father's carpentry business. Everything from tables, roofs, furniture, oxen yokes and more were built by carpenters. Is it any wonder that Jesus would want to keep His ministry impact right where the people congregated daily?

Paul, the apostle, as well as Aquila and Priscilla, were professional tentmakers who also preached the Gospel in the marketplace with great passion. No doubt, God wants us doing the same today.

ZIG ZIGLAR

My dear friend, author, speaker and motivator, Zig Ziglar, said to me just before he passed away, "Staci, I am a preacher that God has used to bring hope to the marketplace, and I believe that is where you are called to shine as well. I am going to send you a book. This book will forever change your career perspective. It is called, *Anointed for Business* by Ed Silvoso. Read it and let it position you early for marketplace ministry."

When that book arrived in my mailbox I opened its pages and read Mr. Ziglar's handwritten words, "God loves you, Staci, and so do I." To some, that may seem like just a simple gesture of kindness, but to me, it was monumental. You see, ever since my father chose to brave the wild and step out of traditional pastoring inside of a church and into sales, Zig Ziglar was his motivator. He read Zig's books like the treasures to success that they really were and eventually made them mandatory reading for my brother and I, too! My dad was the technical editor for Zig's book, *Network Marketing for Dummies*.

Having the privilege of sharing the stage with Mr. Ziglar for over 12 years was one of the most impactful seasons of training in my career. We spoke in front of hundreds of thousands of people during that time, and yet Zig never let the stage or fame move him from knowing that his platform was his pulpit, and his talent to connect with people was a gift from God to the marketplace. Without question, Mr. Ziglar was a marketplace maverick.

As I opened the book, *Anointed for Business*, I was inspired as I read the pages of the introduction that said, "To be anointed for business is to be set aside by God for service in the marketplace. Once anointed, we are to use our job as a ministry vehicle to transform the marketplace so that the gospel will be preached to and heard by every creature in our sphere of influence. The same principle applies in all areas of the marketplace: business, education, and government."

MODERN-DAY MAVERICKS

The search for one's purpose will never be found in titles, bank accounts, relationships, cars or anything that this world could offer. Instead, our life purpose is to be a living vessel of light that God can shine through to the world around us. Millions of people die having never understood their purpose and therefore feel less than fulfilled at the end of their life. I believe that YOU are holding this book so that you will know and surrender to the highest calling of all -- to UNLEASH your full potential on earth and let the Holy Spirit move through you to those around you.

Today, we see modern mavericks popping up to step outside the norm and proclaim their faith and values in the marketplace. One such maverick was S. Truett Cathy, the Founder of Chick-fil-A who passed away in 2014. Cathy decided to close on Sundays in 1946 when he opened his first restaurant in Hapeville, Georgia. Having felt the pressure of working seven days a week, Cathy quickly recognized the importance of closing on Sundays so that he and his employees could set aside one day to rest and worship if they chose to do so. It could mean less profits, or so it would seem. Chick-fil-A, however, has proven a powerful principle in stewardship that when you put God first in all things, God can put you first in everything.

For discussion or meditation:
Who are some other marketplace mavericks that are changing the world?

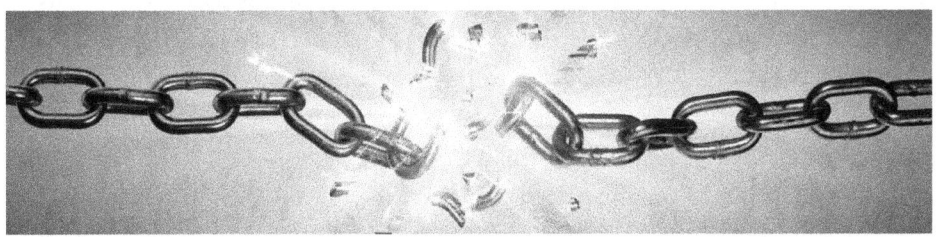

CHAPTER ELEVEN

SUPERHERO COURAGE

In my early 20's, after some notable business successes, I went through a major season of pain and darkness that caused me to learn how to further lean on God and trust in His promises. I was a country music singer and had fallen head over heels for a rodeo cowboy. I was a pure-hearted girl with high hopes, but as our relationship grew, we fell into sin, and I felt trapped by my mistake.

He asked me to marry him, despite being 25 years older than me. I knew it was not God's will for my life, and the voices in my head were screaming for me to walk away, but a soul tie had been formed, and I thought that marrying him would somehow make my mistakes go away. We were only two months into our marriage when a tremendous amount of dysfunction and emotional abuse started taking place. He became more and more possessive and I grew more and more lost, confused and trapped in a marriage that I knew was outside of God's will for my life.

Seven months after our marriage, he filed for divorce, and my heart was crushed. We lived in a state that didn't allow for a contested divorce so for the first time in my life, I felt hopeless, abused and out of control. I thought to myself, "If God ever wanted to use me and my voice, He sure won't now."

That is when I headed full force into suicidal thoughts. Then, one day, as I sat in a state of deep depression and mindlessly flipping TV channels, a lady with pink hair came on the TV and said, "Jesus loves you, and I love you, too." Then she giggled, and I thought to myself, "Why do Christians have to be so weird?" But at that moment, Jan Crouch of the TBN network was precisely who God would use to grab my attention long enough to see the commercial that followed her giggle. It was an invitation to the Believer's Voice of Victory Rally in Ft. Worth, TX.

I was ready to do anything to get back to a place of right relationship with God again. The enemy tried to distract me from that commercial with voices screaming in my head: "You've messed up too much for God to use you now." But I refused those negative voices, and I went to the convention hoping God would somehow meet me there. He did. I heard Gloria Copeland talk about the Bible as if it were more than a book of stories. She said, "It's a book of remedies. If you are sick, look up healing scriptures. If you are sad, look up joy. God has a solution for every situation you are facing."

That day, I realized that God had sent His Word to heal me of my broken heart, my shattered dreams, and my wounded spirit. I went forward at that event and surrendered my life, my talents and my voice to God, saying, "If you can use anything, Lord, use me!" I asked the Holy Spirit to fill me with His presence and to let my life become a conduit of His grace, mercy, and power for the lost and hurting people of my generation.

I moved to Tulsa, Oklahoma and began studying scripture like it was life-sustaining food. I went to church every chance I could, and if there was a special speaker/minister in town, I was there. In that first year, I spent 6-8 hours every day praying, meditating and studying this new life of being totally surrendered to God.

FULLY EMPOWERED

The more I listened, the more I wanted to be like Jesus. I wanted to see people set free, restored, healed and delivered from all their diseases. I wanted to see people gain financial freedom and wholeness: spirit, soul and body. I wanted to be a marketplace maverick fully empowered by the Holy Spirit. As I continued to grow, so did my hunger for the miracle-working power of God. I remember driving home from church one day and was asking God to use my life when I saw a woman get hit by a car while she was walking across the street. The vehicle that hit her was going around 35 miles per hour, and the lady who was hit was heavily intoxicated. I pulled my car over as fast as I could find a spot to stop and ran back to the accident. By the time I got to the woman, a crowd had gathered around her.

> I suddenly became like Wonder Woman pressing through the crowd saying, "Excuse me, I am a minister and I am here to pray!".

What was I saying? I was speaking as if I had done this before and yet, I had only seen it happen through others. Still, I said it over and over, "Please let me through, I am a minister, and I am here to pray." When I got to the woman, she was bleeding from the head, she smelled of alcohol and was in a terrible mess. All I could think about was, "Does she know Jesus?" I was unmoved by her appearance, and I said with absolute certainty, "Ma'am, I am here to pray for you to receive Jesus."

Not knowing how much time she had or if she was going to die right there on the scene, I prayed the most passionate prayer of my life. I prayed that she would know God, accept Jesus as her Lord and Savior and receive His grace and mercy. When I asked if she agreed, she opened her eyes and said, "Yes, yes. Please don't let me die."

At that moment, it was as if I was overtaken by a spirit of absolute authority and boldness when I said, "In the name of Jesus, I command this woman's body to be healed. I speak to these bones to be mended. I command her head to stop bleeding and for every part of her body to line up with the Word of God and that by Jesus' stripes on the cross, she is made whole."

About that time, the paramedics came and took over very quickly. As I stepped aside, I could hear another woman behind me moaning and crying. I turned, and she said, "Did I kill her? Is she dead?" Realizing it was the driver of the car that had hit her, I took her into my arms, and in a completely different spirit of gentleness, I said softly, "Ma'am, I don't know her future, but may I please pray for you?" She immediately put out her cigarette (as if you can't pray and smoke at the same time) and she said, "Yes, please pray."

GENTLE AS A LAMB

There was an immediate spiritual shift in that moment. Instead of a loud lioness voice of boldness, a gentle spirit came over me that was moved by compassion. I prayed for God to give her peace that passes all understanding and to heal her heart from this terrible memory. I prayed for her salvation and then we exchanged numbers and departed shortly after the ambulance left. I spent the rest of that evening reflecting on how quickly that encounter took place and the incredible feeling of knowing that God was using me at that moment. I cried to God, saying, "If you can use anything, Lord, use me."

The next morning, I received a phone call from the lady who hit the wounded woman. She was crying uncontrollably and said, "Did I kill her? Is she dead?" I told her I didn't know, but I would gladly call the hospital and get an update for her. I called the emergency room and the nurse said, "Are you the woman who prayed for her?" I replied, "Yes, ma'am, I am." She responded, "That was the most bizarre incident. We released that woman late last night without injury."

I had uncontrollable tears of joy as I praised God for the miracle of life and I knew, at that moment, that somehow heaven had touched earth and I was privileged to be a witness. That was the first of many miracles that God would enable me to collaborate with Him throughout my life, and it became the bedrock for why I know, beyond any shadow of a doubt, that God is real, God is alive, and God is still doing miracles today.

Luke 4:18 - *"The Spirit of the Lord is on me because He has anointed me to proclaim good news to the poor. He has sent me to proclaim freedom for the prisoners and recovery of sight for the blind, to set the oppressed free, to proclaim the year of the Lord's favor."*

We don't have to be behind a pulpit for God to use us to bring hope to the hopeless and healing to the helpless. God is not looking for perfect vessels; He is looking for willing vessels who hunger and thirst to partner with heaven as it invades earth. God wants to use YOU to be the conduit of healing and miracles today.

For discussion or meditation: Do you believe God can and will do great things in that area so you can be a blessing to others?

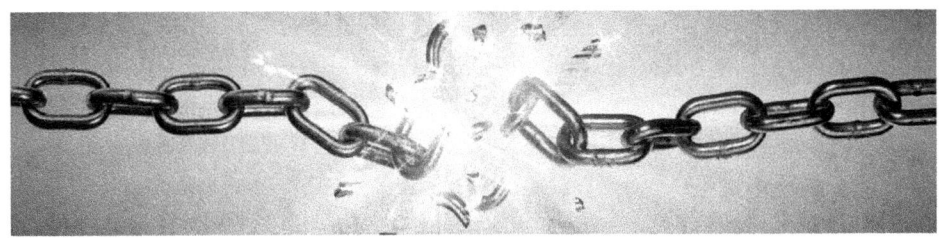

CHAPTER TWELVE

HEAVEN ON EARTH

We serve the Creator of the Universe. He is the only one true God of the miraculous. Whether it is the healing of a major illness, diverting bankruptcy or the restoration of a broken marriage, God has no limitations with His ability to transform our lives and shift the universe on our behalf. Heaven is invading earth every second, every breath we take.

Somewhere, right now, someone is extending the hand of generosity, rescuing the broken-hearted or defending the helpless. When we awaken to a consciousness that God is with and in us, we can begin to sense the greater purpose He has for us.

As I continue to meditate on the magnitude of God using human flesh to be His way of touching people in the marketplace, I realize that ego is the arch-enemy of the miraculous. God partners with our humility, not our pride. That means that we don't have to be perfect, good-looking or famous to be a participant in Heaven's reach.

The more I have longed to see God's presence manifested through my own life, the more I have realized that I had to get out of the way and die to my ego. John the Baptist said it like this, "He must become greater; I must become less." (John 3:30)

SPIRITUAL FASTING

I have found one of the surest way to experience heaven on earth is to silence my ego and reset my focus through prayer and fasting. Spiritual fasting is a time to slow down and become more attuned to God's voice and in alignment with His perfect will for our lives. It's a time of humbling ourselves and subduing our flesh by going without food for a specific period of time.

Why food? The word "fast" or "fasting" in the Hebrew language is "tsom", which means "not to eat." In Greek, it is "nesteia", which means "no food." If we genuinely desire to follow the Biblical model of fasting, it would mean giving up food, which comes with a type of suffering that reminds us of our need for God and His sustenance.

The goal of fasting is to silence our selfish hunger and ambitions, so God can move through us, reposition our hearts and speak to us without interference. (Esther 4:16) Prayer and fasting are power-twins that work together. A fast without sacrificial suffering and prayer is nothing more than self-inflicted starvation.

Matthew 6:16-18 - *"And when you fast, do not look gloomy like the hypocrites, for they disfigure their faces that others may see their fasting. Truly, I say to you; they have received their reward. But when you fast, anoint your head and wash your face, that your fasting may not be seen by others but by your Father who is in secret. And your Father who sees in secret will reward you."*

When I fast, I am crucifying my flesh and setting aside intentional time to pray, freeing my soul from the cares of this world and resetting my focus on the eternal purpose of my existence. In those times of profound meditation on God's greater work in me, I begin to see beyond the physical realm into the spirit world of God's abundant grace, power, and limitless possibilities.

When I find myself falling back into thoughts about my circumstances, talents, ambitions, hurts or concerns, I quickly realize how quickly ego wants to take over and distract me from the divine.

The life of the miraculous, whether we are in a classroom of students, a boardroom of negotiators or in a ballroom of kings, is most greatly expressed through humility and compassion, not ego and self-interest. We live in the place for the potential of heaven and earth to collide around us.

This earth is filled with darkness, hatred, greed, sin, immorality, anger and division. Heaven is calling on ordinary people who have an extraordinary hunger to be used by God to reach this dark and hurting world of humanity.

MOTHER TERESA, A MODERN-DAY MAVERICK

Mother Teresa longed to be used by God to reach those in need. Even as a nun, she was a maverick in that she didn't want to stay confined behind the walls of a monastery, but she so profoundly longed to be on the streets of Calcutta, in the marketplace, with the hurting people. It was unconventional for a nun to "take it to the streets" but that is what was so revolutionary about her ministry. She became the hands and feet of Jesus to the most suffering of humanity. The day she received her Nobel Peace Prize, she quoted the words of St. Francis of Assisi:

"Lord, make me an instrument of your peace;
where there is hatred, let me sow love;
where there is injury, pardon;
where there is doubt, faith;
where there is despair, hope;
where there is darkness, light;
and where there is sadness, joy.
O Divine Master, grant that I may not so much seek to be consoled as to console;
to be understood, as to understand;
to be loved, as to love;
for it is in giving that we receive,
it is in pardoning that we are pardoned,
and it is in dying that we are born to Eternal Life. Amen."

Perhaps, you, too, are called to take His message beyond your cubicle, beyond the door of your office, outside of your church and into the streets of the marketplace around you.

Your life, connected with God, becomes a pipeline of possibilities. You also become His conduit of love, hope, joy, salvation, and healing to those you encounter. Your life takes on immediate significance as you become UNLEASHED as God's special agent of change to this world. What once seemed impossible on your own, suddenly, with God, becomes possible. (Matthew 19:26)

As you grow daily in your intimate connectedness with the Creator of the Universe, you will begin to see that He wants to unleash you and do great things through you. Alignment with God is in alignment with infinite potential. If you have never accepted Jesus Christ as your Savior and Lord, and you want to align yourself with Him today, say this prayer and mean it with your whole heart:

Pray this prayer: "Dear Lord Jesus, I know that I am a sinner, and I ask for Your forgiveness. I believe You died for my sins and rose from the dead. I repent of my sins and surrender absolute control of my life to You. I vow to follow You for the rest of my life and give you permission to pursue me with your love and correction. Fill me with your Holy Spirit and help me to be more like You, in Jesus' name, Amen."

(If you've prayed that prayer, repented of your sin, and have never been baptized in water, I encourage you to contact a leader of faith and tell them you are ready to do so immediately! You will never be the same!)

For discussion or meditation:
What areas of your life do you need to surrender so God can flow through you more freely?

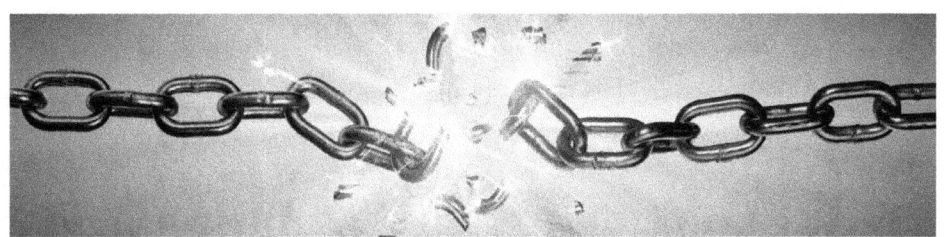

CHAPTER THIRTEEN

THIS IS WAR

There is a war raging, right now, all around us. It is in our homes, our schools, our streets and throughout the marketplace. It is real. It is deadly, and its carnage is evident by the hatred, immorality, division, and selfishness that permeate our society. The battle we face in the marketplace is not a battle of wills or egos inside boardrooms, courtrooms or classrooms. It is a battle in the heavenly realm and only through the power of God's Spirit will we truly be able to take dominion over darkness in the marketplace.

Ephesians 6:10 (NIV) - *"For our struggle is not against flesh and blood, but against the rulers, against the authorities, against the powers of this dark world and against the spiritual forces of evil in the heavenly realms."*

Jesus' life was a living example of how to wage war in the streets of the marketplace. He taught us how to take dominion over principalities, demons, sickness, disease, and temptations of every kind. His entire public ministry lasted only three years, but in that time, He led by example, training and equipping his Motley Crew of disciples daily. He offered them a full-immersion course, a step-by-step clinic on "how to" bring heaven to earth through miracles, healing, deliverance, and victory over sin.

Even though Jesus' hands-on, personal coaching techniques that included visual lessons and storytelling, it was apparent that the disciples were slow in getting the big picture. God was showing them that a massive shift was taking place and soon, they would be the primary conduit for miracles and salvation on earth. In His final days, Jesus "briefed" (to borrow military intelligence terminology) His crew repeatedly about the Master Plan on how they would soon be empowered by the Holy Spirit to take His mantle and mission to GO into all the world.

John 16:7-8 - *"I tell you, it is for your good that I am going away. Unless I go away, the Advocate, the Holy Spirit will not come to you; but if I go, I will send him to you."*

SHIFT HAPPENS

Jesus shifted His ministry from being a "watch and learn" experience into a Spirit-empowered "Go and tell" ministry. Upon sending the Holy Spirit, He transferred authority to anyone who believes, saying, "Go into all the world and preach the gospel to all creation. Whoever believes and is baptized will be saved, but whoever does not believe will be condemned. And these signs will accompany those who believe: In my name they will drive out demons; they will speak in new tongues; they will pick up snakes with their hands; and when they drink deadly poison, it will not hurt them at all; they will place their hands on sick people, and they will get well." (Mark 16:15-18)

What does that mean for you and me? It says that we, too, are called to follow in Christ's footsteps and example, and continue His work wherever we go. It says that we must get out of our seats and into the streets and become the conduits of healing, salvation, and miracles.

> Being like Christ means that we can expect to face principalities that will try to stop us from being effective at work, home and in the marketplace.

Have you ever had the feeling that someone in authority is holding you back from being promoted? Have you ever had someone at work that gets under your skin? Or what about the times when you and your spouse hit an impasse? Perhaps you tried to reconnect with words, flowers, kind gestures or creative antics, but you couldn't seem to repair the canyon of separation between you. These are just a few examples of spiritual battles that require a spiritual response.

PRINCIPALITIES IN THE WORKPLACE

I'll never forget a time when I was involved in a massive clash of personalities with another executive leader in one of the companies where I worked. This leader was determined to be at odds with me, no matter what I did to tolerate and appease him. I had no proof of his intent, but I just knew something wasn't right in our relationship and it seemed there was a spiritual force of darkness all around him. I continued to pray for God's wisdom to reveal any principalities of darkness that would try to stop me from doing what God had called me to do for that company.

Then, one day, I called him to discuss a client I was serving. He was bullish and demeaning in his tone with me, and I thought, "Dear God, help me with this guy and give me patience not to say something I will regret later!"

When he hung up the phone, he accidentally pushed the speaker button instead of ending the call which allowed me to hear into the room. He proceeded to speak harshly about me to someone in his office, using foul names like I had never heard. As I listened to the conversation from my phone for about 30 seconds, I was dumbfounded and everything within me wanted to scream. But the soothing voice of the Holy Spirit said, "Be gentle. Be broken. Let him know you are listening."

I calmly said, "Uhhh...Bill, I am still here on the phone." I waited but there was only silence. I could imagine the look on his face, as well as his blood pressure that was probably "off the charts' at that moment. Immediately, I knew I had him in "checkmate," and my guardian angels had shifted the spiritual environment on my behalf. I continued by saying, "I'm so sorry to hear these words from you and even more sorry for the implication this means to our company."

Come to find out, this wasn't the first or even the worst situation that the company had encountered with him. Not long after this incident, he was released from his position, and God used my calm demeanor in the situation to create favor and respect in a way I could have never set up in the natural realm.

This story is an excellent example of how principalities can be released in a company or home and stagnate growth due to internal conflict. Had I fought only with words or anger, I would have never seen progress. This applies to marriages, friendships, corporate contracts, and even negotiations. Make sure you are fighting a GOOD fight of faith and not a battle of words. (I Timothy 6:11-12 NLT)

When we sense that there is a force set against us, we should never look at the person across from us and engage in a fleshly battle. Instead, we must look up and recognize that this is a battle we must fight in the Spirit. If we try to win the battle with words, we will set ourselves back and potentially destroy the relationship. Instead, we wage war in the Spirit and pray for wisdom that allows God to shift the outcome in our favor.

For discussion or meditation: Can you think of a time when you knew forces were fighting against you, your family or business?

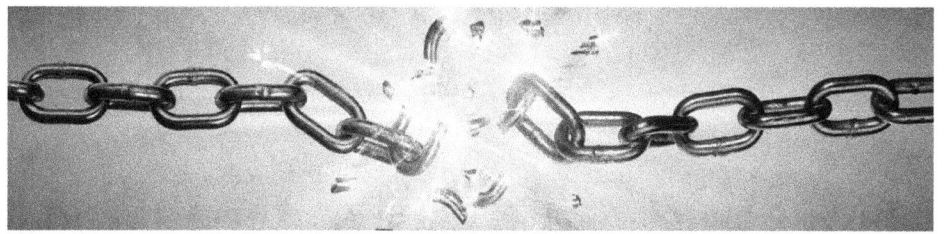

CHAPTER FOURTEEN

EMBRACING CHANGE

In order to see a revival of transformation sweep through our streets, homes, workplaces, and communities, we must be willing to surrender to God and embrace change so that we become more like Christ. Too many Christians are wearing the Jesus t-shirt but not living the Jesus Life. What Jesus was teaching was more than a "one and done" event of having people raise a hand during a church service or say a short prayer of salvation and then send them on their way.

Instead, new believers were continually discipled to be like Jesus, leave their old life, and become living reflections of His nature. As believers became more and more like Jesus, they began to see the results Jesus saw. This progression was seen as His followers began to lay hands on the sick, cast out demons, and speak the truth in boldness so that notable change would be seen in the lives of each believer. This process is what we call the E4 Model of discipleship and a journey every Christian is called to encounter. (E4 = Embrace, Educate, Equip and Empower)

EMBRACE – This is the initial phase of being fully accepted by God, just as you are, sin and all. The minute that you repent, call on the name of Jesus, and are baptized into a new life in Christ, everything begins to change.

Your old life dies and your new life in Christ begins. God breaks into the wretchedness of your world and removes the scales from your eyes that once blinded you to sin. Once that takes place, light begins to force out the darkness in your life. Your old ways of doing things become unfortable and the Holy Spirit draws you into a brand new life. (2 Corinthians 5:17)

When the teachers of the Law brought the woman, caught in adultery, to Jesus, He exemplified what it means to love the lost so they could repent and embrace change. Instead of condemning her, He offered her an exchange when He said, "Neither do I condemn you. Now, go and sin no more." By embracing her as a sinner, right where she was, God was extending the same everlasting and unconditional love that we would be asked to extend to others. He was also topping it off with an explicit instruction that transformational change in her habits and lifestyle should follow.

Turning away from sin is what we call repentance, and it is the foundational phase for every believer and the baseline of Christianity. "Repent and be baptized in the name of Jesus." (Acts 2:38) Repentance is an equity exchange of love between you and Christ. He embraces you just as you are, and in exchange, you turn to him and leave your old life of sin. Not only must you surrender to this new life in Christ, but you will be asked to embrace others just as God embraces you.

> Your role in the marketplace is to love the unlovable, touch the untouchable and be a source of God's healing power and deliverance to those in need around you.

Loving others who are trapped in their iniquity will not always be easy, but Jesus didn't send His Son as a sacrifice for the healthy believers of this world. He sent His Son for those who are still spiritually sick and in need of a great physician. (Mark 2:16-17)

BRAND NEW LIFE

Perhaps God is challenging you to surrender to a new life in Christ today through repentence and baptism. Or maybe you've already done that, and now He wants you to be His voice, hands, and feet to others. Ask God to show you who needs His touch through you. Take time to have lunch with someone at work who others avoid. Next time you go to the mall, ask God who you can pray for or who needs a word of encouragement. People need to know that God is real and His grace covers a multitude of sins. He will embrace us even while we are still caught in bondage to sin, but He uses people, like you and I, to make that connection with others.

My first music CD was entitled *Brand New Life*. I wrote the songs on that CD, shortly after God healed my broken heart. A minister heard my story and said, "Staci, it's time you allow God to turn you mess into a message." That morning, he encouraged me to start writing my own music and allow the Holy Spirit to turn the tests of my past into a testimony for my future. I had never written a full song in my life. After breakfast, he prayed for me, and I felt something shift in my spirit. I went home, and within three short weeks, I wrote 22 songs.

Many of those songs were featured on my first CD, *Brand New Life*. One of the songs I wrote was entitled *Just As You Are*. Consider the words of this song for yourself as well as for those who need to be embraced right where they are today.

JUST AS YOU ARE

Finally, I come before you, ashamed of all the things I've done
So many promises left broken, I can't believe what I've become
I know I don't deserve your love and I've failed to see
No matter how I've let you down you're still reaching out to me
Come unto me just as you are
Though your sins like scarlet flow I'm going to wash you white as snow
Come unto me just as you are
Trust my words and sin no more, come now…just as you are.

In this first EMBRACE phase of spiritual renewal, a sign of your true awakening to this new life will be a natural hunger to know more about God, His ways, and His Word. Perhaps join a small group or Bible study and find a local body of believers that can mentor you through God's Word on a daily basis. Begin to read your Bible consistently. My personal preference for getting started is the Gospel of John. He emphasizes the love of God as found through the life of Jesus Christ. As you read the first chapter of John, you will discover that it opens with God's plan for man even before the creation in Genesis 1.

No matter how you pursue God in this first phase, know that He is pursuing you and will be your closest ally as you begin this new life.

For discussion or meditation:
How often do you read your Bible and spend quality time learning more about the Jesus Life? Have you truly repented and been baptized in the name of Jesus?

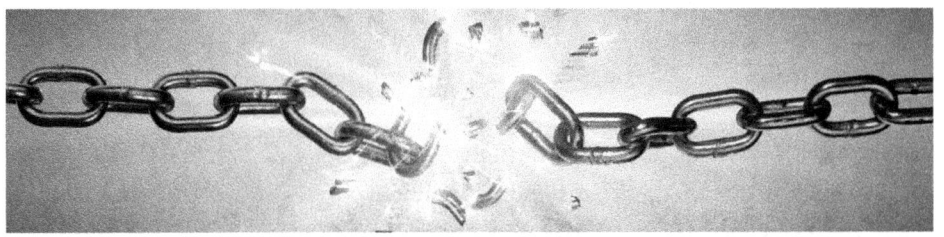

CHAPTER FIFTEEN

GROW UP!

God loves you just as you are, but He also loves you too much to leave you there. In your role in the marketplace, you will discover that God is less impressed with your works and more impressed with your heart of worship and willingness to grow as a better reflection of His character and conduit of His power.

EDUCATE – This is the second phase where we learn to know God's voice, obey His Word, and become His devoted follower. This phase is where we truly learn the value of what it means to be a leader worth following.

The process of changing from our old life into the brand-new life Christ offers us is not an overnight event, but a process of a lifetime that is made possible by the Holy Spirit living IN us. Jesus' disciples and followers were living examples of this progressive metamorphosis.

As we move from the need to be merely embraced and accepted by God, our spirit begins to hunger for more of His likeness. As a baby follower of Christ, you will crave milk, which is usually supplied by simply attending the teachings of others, whether it be in a Bible study, local church, or through the wisdom of other great teachers. Basically, you sit and listen to someone else teach you the principles of God. They do the studying and work, and you drink it in and come back for more week after week. This is infant development in the kingdom.

When I gave birth to my son, Payton, very quickly he became a sucker, meaning he LOVED to be breastfed and would suck all day if I let him. (He doesn't like me telling this story to his buddies, but it's true!). Years later, at the age of 17, I was talking to him about leading others in their walk with God. I was explaining that his maturity in Christ should be transitioning from a consumer mentality into becoming a provider of nourishment to others.

The best example I could think of at that moment was that of breastfeeding. I told him that when he was a baby, he relied on me to eat healthy food so that it would be assimilated into quality breast milk he could drink from me. (As you can imagine, he cringed at this analogy, but I continued.) I explained that drinking nutritious milk from your mama was made possible because she ate specific foods and then passed the nutrients along through her milk.

FROM MILK TO MEAT

But as we mature, milk from a mother is not enough for our muscular development and maturity. We need solid foods. That is what it means to GROW UP in the faith. Instead of our primary intake coming from a pastor, priest or another leader, we need to dig into the Word of God ourselves and get MEAT that begins to change us, strengthen us and mold us into a better reflection of Christ. Paul, the Apostle, was extremely frustrated with the lack of spiritual maturity in the Corinthian church.

1 Corinthians 3:1-4 MSG - *"I'm completely frustrated by your unspiritual dealings with each other and with God. You're acting like infants in concerning Christ, capable of nothing much more than nursing at the breast. Well, then, I'll nurse you since you don't seem capable of anything more. As long as you grab for what makes you feel good or makes you look important, are you much different than a babe at the breast, content only when everything's going your way?"*

Growing in spiritual maturity is the second phase of transformation for all who hope to be unleashed to rule and reign in the marketplace. Much like the process of a caterpillar going through metamorphosis, your personal transformation happens as your mind, will, and emotions begin to conform to God's perfect will for your life.

TRANSFORMATIONAL CHANGE

Romans 12:2 says, *"Do not conform to the pattern of this world, but be transformed by the renewing of your mind. Then you will be able to test and approve what God's will is—his good, pleasing and perfect will."*

> No matter what your past may look like, God wants to transform you into the image of Christ, through the power of the Holy Spirit.

Paul, also known as Saul of Tarsus, wrote this scripture and he knew, first-hand, the transformational change Jesus can offer no matter how wretched our past might be. Paul was a hateful, murderous, unforgiving Pharisee. He sought to kill Christians and was living his life to eradicating Christianity.

Then, one day, Paul was blinded by a light on Gis way to persecute more Christians. Jesus appeared to Him and offered Him unconditional love and a plan to partner with Him to spread the message of Christianity throughout the world. Talk about a reckless and risky love.

Love is the essence of God's gift of sending His only begotten Son. Love, mercy, and compassion are the keys that unlock the miraculous move of the Holy Spirit in the marketplace. Paul had to be re-educated to discover scripture through the new lens of God's love and grace for all humanity. He had to learn to lay down his old life, his opinions, his sin and his ego to serve the eternal lives of others.

Perhaps you, like Paul, have spent your entire life with a skewed perspective on Christianity. Now is a time to surrender your intellect, your talents and your past perspective to God so that He can make you a new creation for His higher purposes. When you do this, you will begin to experience a new life, and you will start to see everything from a fresh perspective.

2 Corinthians 5:17 (NLT) - *"Anyone who belongs to Christ has become a new person. The old life is gone; a new life has begun!"*

Paul's spiritual growth process was not an overnight transformation. Instead, God kept working on Paul long after he left the desert and began his ministry. Discipleship is a journey, not a destination and it's similar for every believer. You start as a child on milk and eventually learn to eat the meat of the Word, growing in strength, wisdom, and stature before man and God.

Perhaps you have gone to a local church community your entire life, and you think you are doing good to sit there and listen once a week to someone spoon-feed you God's Word. Maybe you've even taken a role as a greeter or usher, thinking you are doing your Christian duty to serve the local body.

Chances are you've also attended Bible studies for years and are proud of yourself for being so faithful as a participant of such a holy time of fellowship. While that is acceptable for new believers and should be prioritized as you grow in the faith, God doesn't want you to remain an infant, needing a bottle of milk or simply surrounding yourself with believers.

> God wants you to mature in your faith.

God wants you to grow up in such a way that you don't just "attend" gatherings that feed you, but He wants you to begin studying the Word of God for yourself. He wants you to go from being a student to becoming the teacher.

Hebrews 5:12 - *"By this time you ought to be teachers, but you still need someone to teach you the elementary truths of God's word all over again. You need milk, not solid food! Anyone who lives on milk, being still an infant, is not acquainted with the teaching about righteousness. But solid food is for the mature, who by constant use have trained themselves to distinguish good from evil."*

STEP UP AND STEP OUT

It's time for you to start leading others. You should be leading your family in daily devotions, connecting with co-workers to help them mature in their faith, praying for the sick or starting a Bible study of your own. I can't imagine trying to be an effective wife, mom, business executive, author, and an entrepreneur without the voice of the Holy Spirit helping me grow daily so I can give out of the storehouse of my heart.

HOW TO GROW

1. **Spend time each day reading the Bible and listening to God's voice.** Perhaps download a good Bible app and begin a reading plan. Or, start with a Proverbs each day as well as a chapter from Luke and Acts. Proverbs is a book of wisdom nuggets. Luke is an overview of the Gospel or Life of Jesus Christ and Acts is the book that teaches us how to live a Spirit-empowered life.

2. **Start a small group** of at least two people and hold each other accountable in your faith journey. Practice sharing God's Word with others at work, during a lunch hour, at the gym or while meeting for coffee. (An excellent Bible study to start with is my devotional, *Mission Possible,* as it encourages you to get out of your comfort zone and share your faith like Jesus commanded. Use the videos and audios to help you lead your first small group. Visit: StaciWallace.com/Mission-Possible to get started.)

3. **Attend a weekly gathering of other Christians**, take notes during the message, and then go home each week, study the message for yourself and apply it daily so that it becomes MEAT you can deliver to others.

4. **Pray daily.** (EMwomen.com/Pray)
Begin your prayer time with thanksgiving and praise for what God has already done in your life. Recognize His greatness. Ask Him to supply your needs and finish your prayers by honoring Him as the supreme authority in your life. (Matthew 6)

For discussion or meditation:
What can you do this week to take a step out of your comfort zone of milk and begin to be a meat eater?

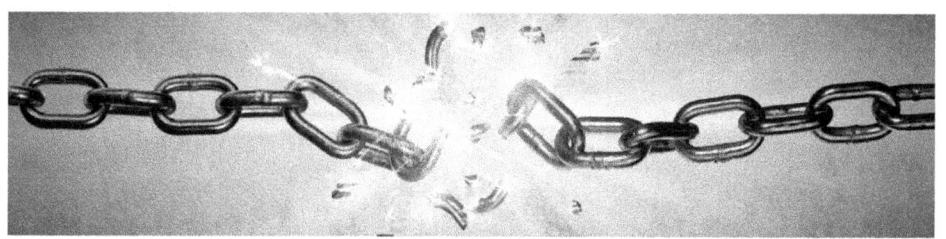

CHAPTER SIXTEEN

THIS NEW LIFE

E QUIP - In this third phase of spiritual renewal, God begins to turn your story into a powerful testimony. He takes your mess and turns it into a message by giving you a new life in Christ. The sins that once held you captive, no longer enslave you because you have been redeemed and set free from bondage. Your identity totally changes. You are no longer that old person you used to be. You are new creation with a new life. To be equipped means you turn to God, not just momentarily due to an emotional need, but with your whole life as a commitment to allow Him to change you from the inside out. This means that you repent, are baptized, and are filled with the Holy Spirit. This is what it means to be born again.

When you are truly born again, everything changes. Your identity changes. Your desires begin to change. Your hunger for the things of God increase. Your willingness to boldly follow the life and example of Christ become your top priority. Why? Because you now have the supernatural power of Christ living in you and His Spirit helping you transform into the image of God.

Being a Christian is so much more than going to church once a week, or emotionally raising your hand at a special service. In fact, the word

Christian was never used by Jesus and didn't surface till a decade after his death. One of the results of being born again is that your faith takes on an active role and you begin to transform into the image of Christ. Faith should lead to renewal. The Bible makes it clear that faith without works is dead. Faith without transformation is dead. Faith without action is dead, and a faith that cannot be seen is not true faith.

"What good is it, dear brothers and sisters, if you say you have faith but don't show it by your actions? Can that kind of faith save anyone? Suppose you see a brother or sister who has no food or clothing, and you say, "Good-bye and have a good day; stay warm and eat well"—but then you don't give that person any food or clothing. What good does that do? So you see, faith by itself isn't enough. Unless it produces good deeds, it is dead and useless." (James 2:14-17 NLT)

The first thing faith should cause you to do is repent and want to turn your old life over to God. This is what makes you stop living in sin like you once did before you surrendered your life to Christ. It shows fruit that you truly are a Christian or follower of Christ.

Think about all of the people sitting in church every Sunday who think that attending church is what it means to KNOW God. Perhaps they've said a special prayer at a service, but they still suffer inside due to continued sin, oppression, addiction, or moral failures. Many have accepted Jesus mentally as their Savior, but have never surrendered their life to Him as Lord of their habits and choices.

A notable Pharisee, Nicodemus, came to Jesus who looked at him and said, "Nicodemus, you need to be born again." (John 3:3-5). That statement confused Nicodemus. Why would he need a spiritual conversion since he was already a religious leader? Maybe you attend church on Sundays and even volunteer regularly, but you still feel like there must be more to this Christian life than you are experiencing. You still operate with old habits and old addictions. You want freedom but you keep going back to your old ways. Nicodemus fasted two days a week, spent two hours every day in prayer, and he was faithful in his tithes and service to the people. When Jesus said, "Nicodemus, you must be born again.", it was because Jesus knew there was more to this life than just knowing about God's laws and following traditional rituals. To be born again means your old man dies and your new life begins.

Jesus saw that Nicodemus was covering his empty soul with religious duties but was lacking a full conversion experience. Nicodemus lacked the love of Christ and therefore lacked an identity IN Christ and in the Kingdom of God. Knowing scriptures and going to church is not what it means to be born again. When you have Christ's love in you, resentment, offense, pride, ego, cursing, anger and addiction become very uncomfortable.

To be born again, means you have the heart of Christ and your nature begins to reflect His nature. You take on the character of Christ and become an ambassador the Kingdom of God on Earth. So many people go to church on Sunday but live like the world every other day of the week. When you are truly born again, "God gives you a new heart and puts a new spirit within you." (Ezekiel 36:26). To be born again is to exchange your old ways for a new life in Christ. It's God's way of giving us a brand new ending to our old story. Here's another way to look at it:

Imagine you had a chance to trade your old car in for a brand new Lamborghini Aventador. Pretty sweet, right? Now imagine taking the new car home and locking it in a garage and never taking it out for a ride. Why on earth would anyone keep a Lamborghini hidden in a garage forever? Unfortunately, that is precisely what people do when they receive Christ but don't display his character or heart. They never share his message or power with others but they simply go about life as if nothing happened. Inside, there is a royal calling, but instead of rising to the occasion of being a royal Ambassador, they stay stuck in their old ways as if they are still driving the same old car.

WATER BAPTISM

Water Baptism is the beginning of your new story in Christ and the initiation of engaging the Holy Spirit's power over your circumstances. It is where the scene of your life changes and your most exciting chapters begin. Water baptism is a powerful burial process that takes place in water. We hold baptisms in lakes, pools, hot tubs, ponds, bathtubs or any location where one can be immersed in water. As you go down into the water and are baptized, you are burying your old, sinful nature into the water with Christ. When you arise out of the water, you are coming up into a brand new life, full of the Holy Spirit and reborn with a new story to tell.

The moment you come up out of the water, you take on a new nature with God's Holy Spirit living in you. Your old spirit literally dies and God's Spirit is alive in you. This is why change should be the evidence of one who has been born again. The Holy Spirit comes in and takes residence in you, equipping you with the power to live a life free from sin.

Water Baptism is not merely a "symbol" of your salvation as many denominations teach. Instead, this is an actual transformational exchange where you surrender your old man and get a new life in Christ. God doesn't just give you a fragmented piece of Himself, but Holy Spirit fills you according to your capacity.

Here's what that means; If someone decided to bless you with brand new furniture for your home, chances are you would need to get rid of some of your old furniture to make room for the new. Similarly, our bodies are the new residence of the Holy Spirit where we allow the Holy Spirit to occupy all of the rooms in our house. The challenge comes when those rooms are already occupied by your old habits and sins that are still taking up space. In the same way, the Holy Spirit wants to fill your life with new habits, desires and power. As you begin to liquidate the old life, you will begin to identify with the NEW YOU and the new freedom that comes with your new identity.

NEVER THIRST AGAIN

In John 4, Jesus came to a well in Samaria and met a woman with a very shady and sordid past. Jesus was about to rewrite her story's ending to what could have been a life of suffering, shame, and tragedy. This woman had been married five times, and the man she was currently living with was not her husband. When Jesus met her, He told her that if she would receive His Spirit that He would fill her with living water that would never run dry. Instead of living in sin and searching for someone to fill her empty heart, Jesus was saying, "Let me come in and give you a brand new life!" (John 4: 10-14 MSG) This woman left the well that day and became a disciple of Christ, telling her community all about the man who set her free. Her scars became stars that lit the way for others to know Christ.

When Jesus spoke of living water, He was referring to the Holy Spirit, Who comes to cleanse us from sin. In my Bible Study Course, *Mission Possible,* I use the analogy of your life being like a tall, clear glass. Imagine that inside that glass are all kinds of rocks that represent the many sins, bad habits and addictions like pride, anger, unforgiveness, sexual immorality, bitterness, envy or a list of any other wrongdoing. If your glass is full of those rocks or funk, then they are taking up space in your life, limiting the capacity for the amount of water it can hold. The water represents the Holy Spirit, His wisdom, and power. When He comes into your life, He only takes up the amount of space that you have the capacity to receive. Immediately, He starts to work on your life to remove the rocks of sin so He can have more freedom to flow through you. He wants less of YOU so that He can give you more of His nature, His power, and His peace. (John 3:30)

As you begin to remove those rocks of sin, it creates more space for the Holy Spirit to come into your life in a more significant way. The more you allow the Holy Spirit to fill your glass over and over, the cleaner the water becomes until, eventually, when someone looks into the glass, they don't see the "funk" or issues of your life anymore. Now, all they see is the crystal clear water. They see Jesus. They see the Holy Spirit. They see God! And thus, you become a reflection of God, and your story takes on a new ending.

EVERY PERSON HAS A STORY AND WHEN REDEEMED, EVERY STORY CAN CHANGE THE WORLD

When God equips you for service, one of the greatest weapons He gives you is your story of forgiveness and healing. You no longer have to be ashamed of your past because God wants to use you, every part of you, to reach the world around you. If you let Him, He can turn your story into a sanctuary of hope for others.

For discussion or meditation:
Have you repented of your sins and been baptized/born again? If not, go immediately to a leader and tell them you want to be baptized in the name of Jesus. You don't haved to wait for as special service or location. You need to believe, repent and submerge your old life in exchange for a new life in Christ.

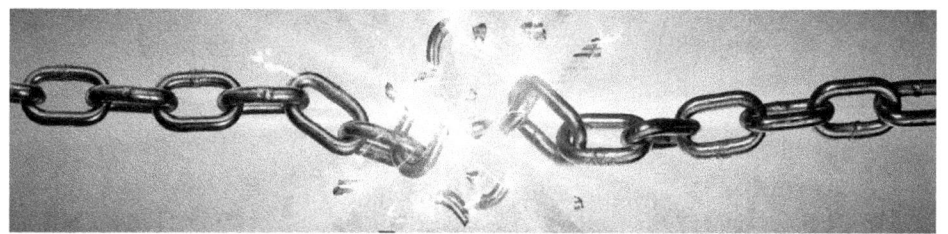

CHAPTER SEVENTEEN

THE FORCE AWAKENS

There is a force of power that comes with being filled with the presence of the Creator of the Universe. When you choose to give your time, talents and treasure to God, inviting His Spirit to dwell in you, something remarkable takes place. You receive power that can only be described as "out of this world".

"You will remove these restraints and leave with the cell door open." These are the famous words of the young girl, Rey, in the Star Wars movie, *The Force Awakens*. In this scene, Rey is bound, hand and foot, in a prison cell awaiting her death while being guarded by an enemy stormtrooper. This is the first time that we see Rey recognize that she is not just an average girl but that there is something more inside her that has not yet been discovered.

At first, she attempts to take authority over the stormtrooper, but she speaks reservedly with fear and trepidation saying, "You will remove these restraints and leave with the cell door open."

The stormtrooper replied: "What did you say?" Again, Rey trembling in fear responds: "You WILL remove these restraints and leave with the cell door open."

Knowing his dominion over her, the stormtrooper grows angry and declares, "I will tighten those restraints, you scavenger scum!"

It is then that Rey recognizes the FORCE within her and boldly proclaims with authority: "You WILL remove these restraints and leave with the cell door open."

Then, the stormtrooper comes into full submission to Rey and obediently replies: "I WILL remove the restraints and leave with the cell door open."

Rey further commands, "And you'll drop your weapon." The stormtrooper fully obeys and she is freed from her captivity.

This scene was my favorite part of the whole movie as I watched the evolution of an ordinary girl who recognizes the power of THE FORCE that lives within her. Rey's awakening continues throughout the movie as she learns how to use "The Force" for good over the enemy.

THE GOD-FORCE

There are millions of people working every day in the marketplace who consider themselves believers in Christ, but they have not fully grasped the power of being filled with the Holy Spirit and what that offers. Instead, they are still under the influence or control of the enemy's strongholds.

The church is filled with many people who struggle with blatant sin. While some of them are growing through the power of the Holy Spirit, others attend church as if it is a social club once a week. Many have never been taught how to be filled with the Spirit so that they can escape a life of bondage to sin.

> When you are baptized in the Holy Spirit, you begin an ongoing filling process that begins to wash out the "old you" and exchange it for a new life in Christ.

Acts 1:8 — *"But you will receive power when the Holy Spirit comes upon you; and you will be my witnesses in Jerusalem, and in all Judea and Samaria, and to the ends of the earth."*

Unfortunately, there has been much division surrounding the person of the Holy Spirit. He longs to have an intimate and personal relationship with you, spirit to Spirit. But like any other friendship, this relationship must be cultivated, matured and given the opportunity to grow.

Not only does that help you win the battle over sin, but it also gives you supernatural power over the enemy to bring God's healing power and deliverance to others.

THREE IN ONE

When someone talks about God as the Holy Trinity, they are speaking of the three roles in which He makes Himself real to us. Much like my dad is a father, a brother and a son, God has revealed Himself to us in three ways. First, He is God, the Father of all creation. Second, He is God, the Son through Jesus Christ. But most personal to us is His role as God, the Holy Spirit, who has come to live in us and empower us to do what Jesus did while He was on earth.

There is only one God, but He reveals himself to us in three ways so that we, as human beings can relate to His omnipotence, personality, and power. Jesus' body was God's earth suit for thirty-three years. He came to live among us and show us how to live the God-life.

The Holy Spirit is the God-FORCE that comes to live in us, giving us a new life in the Spirit and power over the enemy. Holy Spirit is not some far off, mystical ghost, as some imagine. Instead, He is a very close and personal friend to us and is how God makes Himself known to us today.

EMPOWERED BY THE HOLY SPIRIT

EMPOWERED means to give someone the authority or power to do something that they could not do themselves. To be empowered by the Holy Spirit means you are given supernatural abilities to do the work of God on earth.

Jesus' disciples were not powerful enough on their own to overcome sin and live the life of boldness Jesus offered. It took God sending His Spirit to live in the disciples before they became bold witnesses in the marketplace. To be fully empowered to take dominion in the career you've chosen, you will need to be empowered with the supernatural force of the Holy Spirit.

My husband, Larry and I, birthed EMwomen and Epiphany Global to embrace, educate, equip and empower Spirit-filled men and women of God to take the power of the Holy Spirit into all seven mountains of society: including Government, Finance, Health Care or Science, Media & Entertainment, Education, the Family and Religion.

Your life, your job, your talents and your passions all make up the powerful part of how God wants to use you to reach the marketplace around you. Whether your daily activities include teaching, negotiating, parenting, lobbying or volunteering, you need a power greater than your own.

Remember, the battles you will face in this world will not be flesh and blood battles, nor will they be battles of bartering, sales, marketing, or any other form of earthly negotiations. Instead, to indeed gain eternal territory in this life, you will need to wage war in the spirit realm.

In the first chapter of Acts, a doctor named Luke, explains the secret sauce Jesus gave to living an empowered life: "But you will receive power (dunamis) when the Holy Spirit comes on you, and you will be my witnesses in Jerusalem, and in all Judea and Samaria, and to the ends of the earth." The word, dunamis, is used 120 times in the New Testament. It means "the supernatural strength, power and ability of God's nature."

While many believers stop at the salvation, later in Acts Paul tries to explain that God had so much more to offer. He fully understood the empowerment that came through the Baptism of the Holy Spirit and spent his life teaching others of His power.

Acts 19:1-6 - *"Did you receive the Holy Spirit when you believed?" They answered, "No, we have not even heard that there is a Holy Spirit." So, Paul asked, "Then what baptism did you receive?" "John's baptism," they replied. Paul said, "John's baptism was a baptism of repentance. He told the people to believe in the one coming after him, that is, in Jesus." On hearing this, they were baptized in the name of the Lord Jesus. When Paul placed his hands on them, the Holy Spirit came on them, and they spoke in tongues and prophesied."*

The empowerment of the Holy Spirit is well recorded throughout the Book of Acts, and it includes miracles, signs, wonders, and deliverance. Peter healed a lame man (Acts 3:1-11) and raised the dead (9:36-41). The apostles performed many supernatural miracles, signs, and wonders (5:12-16) and Paul cast out an evil spirit (16:16-18). These astounding works of the Holy Spirit were for the advancement of the Kingdom of God on earth.

God uses ordinary people just like you and me to make Himself known on the earth. To be filled with the Holy Spirit is a part of the progressive transformation of a believer's life. It's beyond salvation. It's beyond water baptism. It's having an intimate relationship with the Spirit of God where you connect to His power, wisdom, knowledge, and compassion. As your life coach, He will teach you how to pray and how to have a special connection with Him that supersedes anything you've ever imagined. (Romans 8:26, 27)

For discussion or meditation:
Have you been baptized in water and in the Holy Spirit?

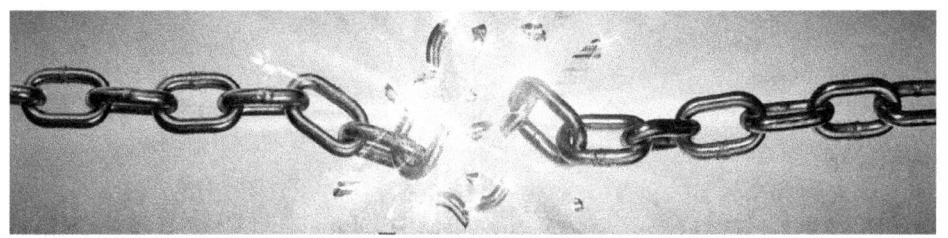

CHAPTER EIGHTEEN

DIRECT CONNECT

"All of them were filled with the Holy Spirit and began to speak in other tongues as the Spirit enabled them." - **Acts 2:4**

When you are "baptized in the Spirit" you are immersed and filled by the power by God's Spirit to do what Jesus did and lead others with the same power, authority, and certainty. That means that His power is in you, but you still need to learn how to use it in your everyday life by growing in wisdom and understanding of your new role and responsibility.

When this happens, something extraordinary takes place. Not only are you given the power to overcome sin, but you are also empowered to lay hands on the sick, raise the dead, cast out demons, be the conduit of God's power on earth and speak to God in a new, heavenly language.

This special enduement of power is not something reserved only for elite Christian leaders, ministers, or pastors. It is for all who believe, and it gives you an extraordinary ability to have a direct connect with God's Spirit and to become His conduit of Heaven on Earth. (Mark 16:17-18)

A PRIVATE LANGUAGE BETWEEN YOU AND GOD

When you are filled with the Holy Spirit, you are given a private prayer language between you and God. It is a spirit-to-Spirit language that scripture calls "speaking in tongues". It's an unknown language based on a believer's faith, not one's intellect and it is different than the "gift of tongues" which is a special spiritual gift given selectively by God.

You are a spirit being having an earth experience inside of a human body. When you speak in tongues, you are engaging your spirit in a personal spirit-to-Spirit communication with God. You may not know what you are saying when you speak in tongues, but God does, and the Holy Spirit makes intercession for you as you pray. This spiritual prayer language it is available to all who believe. Not everyone who is filled with the Spirit, however, uses their spiritual language. Many have been convinced that it is only for a few elect people. But it is a communication of faith that is available to all who believe, are baptized, and filled with the Holy Spirit.

Look at it this way: Your natural language or how you communicate with other people is a mental and physical connection that goes from your mind through your lips to another person. It requires you to open your mouth and speak out before it becomes words that others can hear and understand. Your spiritual language, instead of coming from your mind or intellect, is a spiritual connection that flows from your spirit through your lips to God, who always understands what you are saying.

JUST AS YOUR NATURAL LANGUAGE IS THE VOICE OF YOUR MIND, PRAYING IN TONGUES IS THE VOICE OF YOUR SPIRIT.

It is your spirit speaking to God. The Apostle Paul said, "For if I pray in tongues, my spirit is praying..." (1 Corinthians 14:14 ESV) It's no wonder Satan wants the church divided on this topic. He loves the idea of us NOT connecting with God through our spirit language. When a believer is told that "speaking in tongues is of the devil or not for today," they are being hindered from entering the more profound things of God and limiting their power over darkness.

God knows what you need and how to bring it to pass. He knows how to best position you in the marketplace with wisdom so that He can manifest His power through you on earth. His thoughts are higher than your thoughts, and His ways are higher than your ways. When you "pray in the Spirit," you are not praying according to your will, but you are tapping into His will, His thoughts and His potential for your life.

With all transparency, I battled voices in my head as to whether to include this section in my book. I know it is a controversial topic that splits denominations and religions, which are both institutions created by man. I had voices in my head saying, "Staci, talking about this special power will limit the number of books you sell." But then as I prayed in the Spirit, I sensed a Voice saying, "Staci, if you had the cure for cancer would you not want to tell everyone about it? Even if people didn't believe you, if you knew the truth, wouldn't you shout it from the rooftops so anyone who was sick could be healed? People are settling for man's medicine and looking for man's opinions and cures. But my Spirit, is the source of all power."

Scripture says that when we pray in tongues, we're speaking mysteries to God. We're calling forth parts of God's plan we don't even understand with our natural mind. It is God's way of enabling us to tune into Heaven's airwaves of wisdom and downloading Heaven on Earth guidance.

HEAVEN'S FREQUENCIES

Compare it to turning on a radio. I love listening to a good worship channel when I'm in my car. But if I am sitting comfortably in my garage, it's hard to get the frequency strong enough to hear the channel. It's distorted and quite honestly, frustrating. If I pull out of the comfort zone of my garage, however, my car's radio system can tune in perfectly to receive a strong signal so the music comes through loud and clear. Tuning in to the Holy Spirit works the same way. If you limit Him only to the comfort zone of your intellect, you will restrict yourself from hearing and downloading the deeper things of God. The only way to fully know the things of God is through communion with the Spirit of God.

1 Corinthians 2:9-14 (ESV)- *"But as it is written: "Eye has not seen, nor ear heard, nor have entered into the heart of man the things which God has prepared for those who love Him. But God has revealed them to us through His Spirit. For the Spirit searches all things, yes, the deep things of God. For what man knows the things of a man except for the spirit of the man which is in him? Even so, no one knows the things of God except the Spirit of God. Now we have received, not the spirit of the world, but the Spirit who is from God, that we might know the things that have been freely given to us by God. These things we also speak, not in words which man's wisdom teaches but which the Holy Spirit teaches, comparing spiritual things with spiritual. But the natural man does not receive the things of the Spirit of God, for they are foolishness to him; nor can he know them, because they are only spiritually discerned."*

When we haven't fine-tuned our spirits enough to pick up the voice of the Spirit, we hear a few things now and then, but for the most part, we stay confined to our garage or comfort zones and the signal fades in and out. This is when I hear well-meaning Christians tell me they lack clarity or certainty on a matter. It doesn't mean that God isn't speaking, or the Holy Spirit isn't moving. It just means that we need to reposition our hearts to receive.

Praying in the Spirit (in tongues) is the fastest, most effective method I know of for tuning in to God's voice and gaining perfect clarity on a matter. There have been many times when I have been called upon to enter a room of elite professionals who would intimidate even the strongest of leaders. Before I enter the room, I always surrender my talents, intellect, and will to the Father by taking time to pray in the Spirit. As I do, I sincerely believe that God downloads "mysteries" beyond my understanding, so that when I enter the room, I have an elevated ability to communicate and discern what is needed in that moment. I know in that moment that I can trust the Holy Spirit to speak through me. (Matthew 10:20)

Far too long, we've been satisfied with only preaching the non-controversial scriptures of the Bible. But I know for a fact that praying in tongues has been a secret sauce in my career. It has helped me get out of my own thinking and tune in to what God wants me to say and do in the rooms I am in. I firmly believe there will be an explosion of the power of God when we start to engage the Holy Spirit in our conversations, negotiations and everyday interactions.

For discussion or meditation:

If you desire to receive the Baptism in the Holy Spirit, you can do so right now by simply praying this prayer:

"Heavenly Father, thank you for sending Jesus to be my Lord and Savior. Your Word says that when I ask, I will receive the Holy Spirit. So in the Name of Jesus Christ, I am asking You to fill me to overflowing with Your Holy Spirit. I believe that you have given me this special prayer language to connect with you anytime and anywhere. I now receive this special way of connecting more intimately with you. I will now use my lips to realease sounds or mysteries in an unknown tongue. I fully trust that you know the meaning of the sounds I release as I pray from my spirit. In Jesus name, Amen."

Now, begin to release the sounds that come forth from your spirit. Bypass your mind or intellect and don't let human thoughts or voices try to convince you this isn't real. As the first sound comes out, God hears your spirit and receives your faith.

Thank God and praise Him for baptizing you in the Holy Spirit and for giving you this special prayer language. Spend time praying in tongues daily and you will grow to have your spirit on God's wavelength "at all times". This is how you have a 24/7 connection with the Holy Spirit.

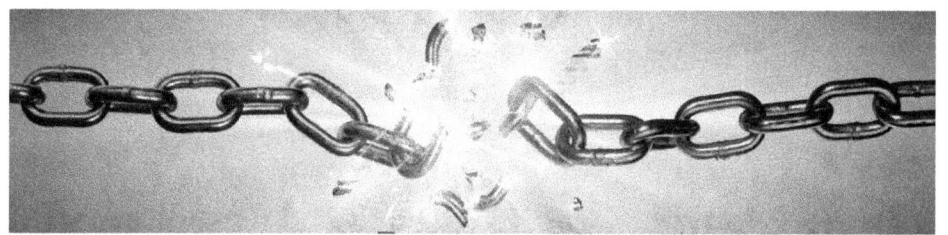

CHAPTER NINETEEN

SPIRITUAL GIFTS

Satan is going to send his deceptive spirits to seduce, bully, perjure, lie, fabricate, manipulate and twist the minds of those who try to disrupt his plan for the marketplace. That is why, as Christians, we need the power of the Holy Spirit and EVERYTHING He offers us to fight spiritual warfare in the marketplace.

Paul was deeply passionate about teaching new believers the importance of the special gifts or abilities that the Holy Spirit provides us to overcome the enemy. These gifts are also what equip us to negotiate beyond our pay grade, manifest miraculous turnarounds in the marketplace, bring God's healing virtue to those who are sick and infuse rooms with elevated wisdom and faith.

1 Corinthians 12:1 (AMP) - *"Now about the spiritual gifts [the special endowments given by the Holy Spirit], brothers and sisters, I do not want you to be uninformed."*

Far too many Christians are uninformed about the things of the Spirit and therefore they have no dominion over their flesh or the spirits surrounding them at home or work. To negotiate territory on behalf of Kingdom purposes, you will need a knowledge and confidence in the supernatural gifts of the Spirit. As you seek God's face, listen to His voice, hunger for His presence and receive the gifts He provides, He will help you execute HIS will on earth.

We are encouraged in 1 Corinthians 12:31 to "earnestly desire" spiritual gifts so that we can be empowered in our jobs, with our families and in every aspect of life.

Even as it relates to conflict resolution, we need the Holy Spirit to guide us. Being a devoted follower of Christ comes with a high probability of opposition as you press AGAINST the grain of the world's system. This is how Paul endured prison, stoning, rejection and physical abuse while sharing his faith. It was only by the power of the Holy Spirit that he could endure and choose to forgive his accusers. Stephen, while being stoned to death, remained in a state of supernatural peace as He said, "Lord, do not hold this sin against them." (Acts 7:60)

Most leaders today would never allow such injustice, but they would seek revenge at all cost. But the lesson of the disciples, apostles and Christ was that there is another way. There is another system of justice and another way to find true and lasting peace and it is through the power of the Holy Spirit.

The apostles showed us that we must unplug from the normal thoughts, patterns or strategies of this world and tap into the supernatural perspective of the Spirit. No matter what financial state the apostles were in, and whether they were being persecuted or bound in chains, they were able to separate themselves from the world's system of greed and power and shift into a heavenly mindset that repositioned their time, talents and treasure from selfish gain into true generosity in their lives for the benefit of others.

Romans 12:2 - *"Do not conform to the pattern of this world but be transformed by the renewing of your mind. Then you will be able to test and approve what God's will is—his good, pleasing and perfect will."*

To do this, we need the gifts of the Spirit in action in our lives. Who can receive the Gifts of the Holy Spirit? As we earnestly seek the Holy Spirit's gifts in our lives, scripture tells us that He freely gives His gifts to all who believe so that we can be a blessing to others. *(1 Corinthians 12:7)*

The Spiritual Gifts in Three Groups

1. Revelation gifts are for insight and include the word of wisdom, the word of knowledge, and discerning of spirits.
2. Vocal gifts are tongues, interpretation of tongues, and prophecy.
3. Power gifts include faith, healing, and the working of miracles.

> Spiritual gifts are specifically designed to empower us with supernatural abilities to help us lead others to Christ and gain victory in our everyday lives.

Whether it is in the marketplace, at our jobs, in our relationships or in ministry, God wants to equip us with His power to perform at a level of supernatural potential for His purposes and His glory.

As leaders, we are called to use our spiritual gifts to take God's power into the world of business where non-believers spend the majority of their time. Since many will never grace the steps of a church, the marketplace is the BEST place for God to use our gifts on a daily basis.

Spiritual gifts can help us discern spirits in boardrooms, hear wisdom that supersedes our pedigree, help us have supernatural knowledge, share hope with those in depression around us and even empower us to shift rooms of impossible negotiations into miraculous turnaround victories. Spiritual gifts will change our posture, perspective, productivity, and people-skills so that we can become a better reflection of God's light and power to the world around us.

Let's take a deeper look at the Gifts of the Spirit and how they operate. First, let's look at the revelation gifts or those that deal with your intellect, understanding and discernment.

REVELATION GIFTS

1. Word of Wisdom: This is supernatural knowledge of God's Word and an understanding on how to apply it to all of life's situations.

The Bible offers the most powerful strategies for business development known to man. There has never been a more strategically duplicated message or highly accepted term sheet than that of the Bible. I like to call it Heaven's Constitution for Earth. If you want massive expansion and growth in your life, business and relationships, THE BIBLE IS YOUR MANUAL FOR SUCCESS and wisdom is your key to understanding it.

Proverbs 3:13-18 - *"Blessed is the one who finds wisdom, and the one who gets understanding, for the gain from her is far better than the gain from silver and her profit better than gold. She is more precious than jewels, and nothing you desire compares with her."*

Having wisdom should be our daily quest. There are many people who have PhD's, impressive pedigrees and who are book-smart beyond measure. But wisdom only comes when we put that book knowledge into action. The same is true when reading the Bible, we can memorize scripture, know all the stories of the Bible and think we've got it all under wraps. But if we do not obey what we read, we are missing WISDOM. To know God's Word and apply it, is the beginning of wisdom. The Gift of Wisdom is a powerful asset in the marketplace as wisdom gives us an ability to make critical decisions when others tend to be caught in paralysis by analysis.

When Jesus was faced with temptations in the wilderness, wisdom helped Him see through the enemy's tactics and He quickly applied God's Word and resisted Satan. Adam and Eve, on the other hand, failed to recognize the enemy's lies and were therefore deceived. Knowing how to recognize the tactics of the enemy and then apply God's Word with authority can mean the difference between life and death.

2. Word of Knowledge: This is supernatural insight given by the Holy Spirit that could not possibly be known without the Holy Spirit's prompting. The Gift of Knowledge helps us understand the undisclosed things of this world and operate at a level of leadership strength that is beyond normal. An example would be in Acts 5:3 when Ananias and Sapphira sold their land and falsely claimed they had given all of the profits to God's work. They were being dishonest in their stewardship, but Peter received a Word of Knowledge that prompted him to boldly ask, "Ananias, how is it that Satan has so filled your heart that you have lied to the Holy Spirit and have kept for yourself some of the money you received for the land?"

This gift sees into the unseen and encourages others to do the will of God. Many with this gift have spent a considerable amount of time studying God's written Word and have memorized scripture so they can effectively communicate it to others spontaneously.

One morning I woke up at 3 am with a picture of my daughter's iPhone in my head. I am used to the Holy Spirit waking me around that time to commune with Him, but this was different. I sensed something was wrong with her phone. As I meditated on it, Holy Spirit revealed that she was doing something on her phone that could be dangerous. When she woke up, we did a "surprise and spontaneous phone check".

As I scrolled through her phone, it all seemed very innocent. Then, I gave it to my husband and he noticed an app that was unfamiliar to us. It was a cute doll-dress-up app that seemed harmless. But then he noticed that it was also a game that allowed communication between players globally. One of her "international" player friends was asking questions like, "How old are you?" "Where do you live?" "What is your favorite color?" Reading further into the week's conversations, we realized that she was speaking with a potential pedophile. We sat down with her and had a very long and serious conversation about online safety and personal privacy.

We were shocked to see how something so innocent could turn destructive so quickly. Our hearts were racing and my "mommy instinct" wanted to ban her from apps forever. But we knew that we can't keep her from evil but we can educate and equip her to know right from wrong in the future. Thank God I listened that morning and thank God for the Gift of the Word of Knowledge. Holy Spirit gives gifts to equip and empower us in everyday situations and life.

3. Discerning of Spirits: The third of the Revelation gifts is the gift to discern spirits and to have an elevated awareness of the circumstances, opposition and people around you. It is a supernatural ability to detect lies and separate truth from fiction.

Have you ever met someone that seemed a bit shady? Perhaps you had to do business with them day after day, but something just didn't seem quite right? Discernment is that inner gut feeling that tells you when someone or something is "off". It may look right and sound right, but you know something is not quite on the up and up. When you have the Gift of

Discerning Spirits, that "feeling" jumps out as a "knowing" that spiritual warfare is taking place against you or those you love.

It was the Gift of Spiritual Discernment that empowered Paul to recognize and cast out the evil spirit from a fortune-teller who was claiming to know and follow God. While others listened to her babble on, Paul rebuked the evil spirit in her by saying, "I command you in the name of Jesus Christ to come out of her. And at that moment the spirit left her." (Acts 16:16-18)

If you accept the call to be a marketplace evangelist, you will, no doubt, come face to face with imposters, liars, hypocrites and people under the influence of demonic spirits. They may be at the top of the charts, winning awards, dazzling the masses, acquiring millions of followers and even singing songs of praise to God, but if their life does not reflect the fullness of God's word, they are imposters.

REAL DELIVERANCE

I was speaking at a church in Modesto, California, a location known for prolific witchcraft and demonic activity. The pastor was young and asked for our team to come and teach on the power of deliverance and miracles.

I began explaining the importance of being filled with the Holy Spirit, as I said, "Luke 11:24 tells us that when you cast out unclean spirits from a person's life, the spirits will search for an empty or arid place to land. In other words, they search for a heart that is empty or one that is not filled with the Spirit."

Now, let me explain that when I train leaders on the deliverance of unclean spirits, it is an intensive training and not to be taken lightly. However, when a person or group of people are ready to receive, things happen that are out of this world. Within a few short minutes, the female youth pastor in the room started screaming with a man's voice and being thrown around by a demonic spirit. Recognizing the situation, I sternly said to the rest of the room, "This is real people. This is not a drill. If you are not right with God, repent of your sins immediately and invite the presence of the Holy Spirit into your life."

Suddenly, everyone, including the entire church staff, hit the floor crying out to God. I heard them repenting and praying out loud. Meanwhile, the woman with the evil spirit was being tormented and her body was being thrown violently around the room. I commanded her to be still and her body fell to the ground. Then the spirit screamed at me in a man's voice saying, "I won't leave her."

My husband and a few others were helping to hold the woman down to prevent more physical harm. The struggle for this woman's life was real and the spirit was relentless. The woman had been a carrier of the spirit for quite some time. She had participated in seances as a teen and had recently played with Ouija boards after innocently visiting a white witch with a few friends.

When I asked her to declare the name of Jesus as her Savior, she would not obey. I boldly commanded the spirit to loose her and set her free in the name of Jesus. There was silence but a deep groaning beneath her breath. That is when I commanded the young woman to call out the white witch's name and denounced her power. Suddenly, the evil spirit left and when it did, the countenance of this young woman completely changed. After she was freed from the spirit, she professed the name of Jesus and was filled with the Holy Spirit.

PARANORMAL VS. SUPERNATURAL

Today, our generation has best-selling books, movies, games and tv shows that make witchcraft and paranormal activity seem like innocent entertainment. I've watched pastors use Harry Potter examples or rated R movies for their sermon text in front of thousands of people. Clearly, they are ignorant of the deeper things of God's Word. Light and darkness are like oil and water…they are repulsive to one another. The demonic realm is real and so are evil spirits that are invited in when individuals entertain themselves with their lies.

We are in a holy war in the marketplace and we cannot let what appears to be "good" steal from what God has intended to be His BEST in our lives. The gift of discerning of spirits is going to be a powerful asset in taking dominion over darkness in today's world. It operates closely with prophecy and signs and wonders as it aids in the ministry of deliverance of others and helps to protect us from spirits of darkness that come to kill, steal and destroy God's greater work.

For discussion or meditation:

Do you have any items that you need to remove from your home, office or environment that could be opening the door to darkness?

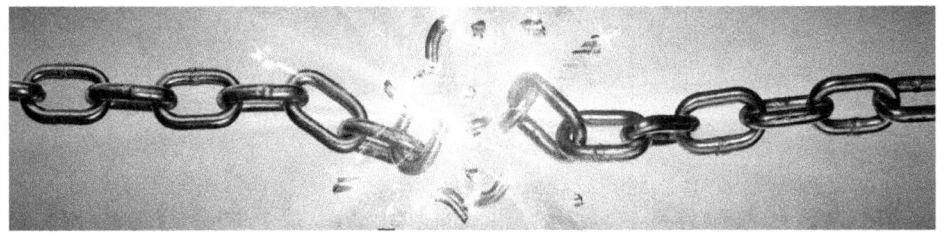

CHAPTER TWENTY

SUPERNATURAL COMMUNICATION

Years ago, my husband and I came across a sci-fi film called, *Arrival*, which is about a female linguist, enlisted by the U.S. Army to communicate with aliens that had come to earth. Her job was to try and figure out their alien language, relay their message to the Army officials, and help stop a potential war.

As I watched the movie, I thought about how humanity has a hunger to find attachment to something "out of this world". We want to believe that there is more to life than what we see and feel on earth. Trillions of dollars are spent to investigate life on other planets. We have an insatiable desire to connect and communicate with greater intelligence than our own.

The term "Supernatural Communication" sounds like something from a sci-fi movie, but in reality, it is exactly what God has given us through the Holy Spirit to communicate with Him directly. The insatiable desire to connect with beings from other planets is really the desire God has placed in us to connect with Him.

1. **The Gift of Tongues:** While prayer is what we do when we use our natural mind and language to talk to God, speaking in tongues is when we

use our spirit language, which without interpretation sounds like jibberish to the human ear. It is our faith-language between us and God. But different that both prayer and speaking in tongues is what scripture calls the Gift of Tongues. In 1 Corinthians 14, it is described as a special "gift of the Spirit" that is given to select members of the Church to intercept and communicate information from God's heart to humanity.

Sounds pretty cool, right? Imagine downloading a message from God in an unknown language and then having it interpreted so people on earth can understand. That is exactly what the Gift of Tongues allows.

HEAVENLY LINGUISTICS

You don't have to be summoned by the U.S. Army or be a Harvard Graduate of Language and Linguistics to tap into the Spiritual Gift of Tongues. It is a gift given by God for the public edification of those who hear it. In fact, educational institutions, pedigrees, or fancy titles alone, have zero power or ability to access or explain this language. For many, if they can't understand it or control it, they simply describe it as foolishness.

Yet scientific research has now documented that while they can't explain it, those who speak in tongues in a private or public manner, have undeniable physical benefits. A study done by the American Journal of Human Biology revealed that speaking in tongues is associated with both a **reduction in circulatory cortisol, and enhancements in alpha-amylase enzyme activity.** These are two common biomarkers of stress reduction that can be measured in saliva.

Without the empowerment of the Holy Spirit, it is untouchable, unrecognizable and foolishness to those who don't believe. It can't be taught or bought. It is supernatural and those who have received this gift are ordinary people that God chooses to give His unfiltered, extraordinary messages to on earth.

Consider the Spiritual Gift of Tongues as God's voice without translation. Before His heavenly language can be understood, it sounds like babbling to the human ear. But when interpreted, it brings life and encouragement to God's people. The New Testament describes this controversial language as a gift used in the church body for awakening believers to the supernatural presence of God on earth.

Paul made himself clear when he wrote, "I would like every one of you to speak in tongues." (1 Corinthians 14:5) Paul knew the power of being able to hear God's messages clearly and directly. But He also knew that for this special gift to edify the people in a public setting, there would need to be an interpretation of the heavenly language to help the people understand what is being said. That is why this gift is to always be partnered with interpretation as to not lead to confusion.

2. Interpretation of Tongues is the supernatural ability to translate the unknown spiritual language of the Holy Spirit.

The only way an outspoken message in tongues is profitable or beneficial to humanity is if it is translated into their understanding. Being able to translate a message of tongues is essential in order that it bring edification and enlightenment to the people listening.

1 Corinthians 14:13-18 - *"For this reason the one who speaks in a tongue should pray that they may interpret what they say." ... (vs. 16) "Otherwise when you are praising God in the Spirit, how can someone else, who is now put in the position of an inquirer, say "Amen" to your thanksgiving, since they do not know what you are saying?"....(vs 18) "I thank God that I speak in tongues more than all of you."*

Paul was instructing the church on how to administer this gift in public settings so that confusion would not enter the hearts of people. (1 Corinthians 14:33) Some people believe the Gift of Tongues and Interpretation is demonic or has passed away with the death of the apostles. But this is just not true and why Paul spent so much time instructing the church about it.

Satan delights when God's people refuse their ability to download spiritual truths through the Gift of Tongues and Interpretation because He knows it is a powerful asset that equips the church, awakens non-believers and empowers God's people.

3. Prophecy is supernatural foresight or revelation given by God to encourage His people and help them live a more abundant life.

1 Corinthians 14:1 (ESV) - *"Pursue love, and desire spiritual gifts, but especially that you may prophesy."*

The Gift of Prophecy is perhaps one of the most important of all gifts, both in the local church and in business. A prophet is a watch-person that sees what other people can't see so they can deliver a message other people need to hear. In a business setting, a leader with a Gift of Prophecy can discern what is needed in their company and see ideas, solutions and concepts that give clarity and wisdom when needed. If corporations, businesses and even family units had this gift in operation, just think how many wrong decisions, faulty partnerships, and divisive conflicts could be diverted.

We see the significance of prophets and prophecy throughout both the Old and New Testament. In the Old Testament, God used prophets to come alongside Kings of power so that they could make the best decisions on behalf of their kingdom. (1 Chronicles 17:1-15) One of my biblical heroines is the prophet and judge, Deborah. Talk about an empowered woman!

Judges 4:4-9 - *"Now Deborah, a prophet, the wife of Lappidoth, was leading Israel at the time. She held court under the Palm of Deborah between Ramah and Bethel in the hill country of Ephraim and the Israelites went up to her to have their disputes decided."*

Deborah was a boss-lady in the highest degree. She gave wise counsel to top leaders. She was the judge over national disputes. And she told armies when to go to battle and how to wage war. She was a great example of how prophecy empowers both men and women to have fierce boldness and courageous leadership.

In the New Testament, the Gift of Prophecy was readily seen in the apostles as they admonished the people to repent, turn to God and experience the love of the Father. In every case, prophecy was for edifying, exhorting and strengthening the people to be better servants of God's will on the earth.

1 Corinthians 14:3-4 - *"The one who prophesies speaks to people for their strengthening, encouraging and comfort. Anyone who speaks in a tongue edifies themselves, but the one who prophesies edifies the church."*

Though prophecy may warn and challenge, it is always for awakening us, comforting us, and encouraging us to live our most excellent life in Christ.

PROPHECY IN THE WORKPLACE

I remember being a top sales leader for a company that was breaking new ground. They had hired an IT industry legend, but I sensed something just wasn't right about his relationship or love for the people. I shared my concerns with the CEO, but this guy's pedigree enamored them.

One night I had a vision that I was walking up to someone's porch when I saw a massive snake in the flower garden. As I looked closer, I saw that the snake's head bore this man's face. When I awoke, I knew this was either a Gift of Knowledge or Prophecy. It was a warning that this highly pedigreed man was the wrong person to be at the helm of IT development. I sensed immediately that his leadership would bring significant harm to the company.

I offered my concerns to the CEO, but he dismissed my warnings as simply "crazy talk." That is often the response shown to those operating with the Gift of Prophecy as the prophet sees what others cannot see. I knew I had obeyed God's leading in sharing the vision and providing a clear warning. Only a few months later, the truth was revealed that this man created technology that was devastating to the future growth and development of the company. It forced millions of dollars in re-engineering the technology and eventually led to the company's demise.

> If modern day kings would surround themselves with proven, God-fearing prophets, I am convinced that the results of these successful companies would skyrocket while bringing greater glory to God.

When we remove God's wisdom from our boardrooms, classrooms, government offices and businesses, we are left with mere human potential that leads to an ego-driven model of man's power devoid of the supernatural.

For discussion or meditation: Do you or anyone you know have the gift of prophecy? Is your company currently surrounded by wise counsel that operates with this Spiritual Gift?

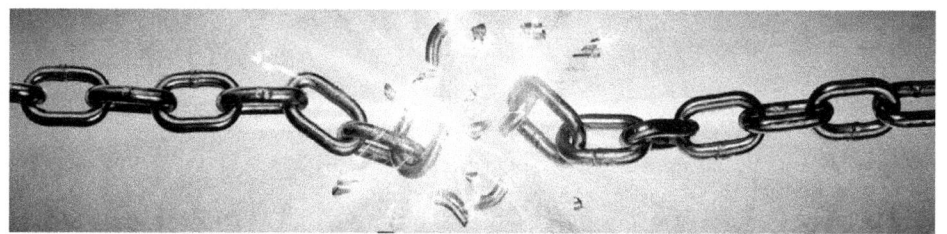

CHAPTER TWENTY-ONE

THE POWER GIFTS

"And these signs will accompany those who believe: In my name, they will drive out demons; they will speak in new tongues; they will pick up snakes with their hands; and when they drink deadly poison, it will not hurt them at all; they will place their hands-on sick people, and they will get well." - **Mark 16:17-18**

Faith is the greatest of the power gifts as it is the key to all other gifts becoming reality. Each one of us were given a "measure of faith" (Romans 12:3) – just enough measure to make it through this life successfully. Mark 11:22 tells us that it only takes faith the size of a mustard seed to move mountains.

1. **Faith:** a supernatural belief in God's Word to do the impossible

Faith is the backbone of all spiritual gifts and the one gift that every believer must have to take dominion in the marketplace today. Faith enables leaders to take calculated risks that others would never think of making. Jesus was trying to explain this to His disciples when they came to Him wondering why they were not yet able to cast out evil spirits. He told them it was because of their lack of faith.

> **Matthew 17:19-22** - *"Then the disciples came to Jesus in private and asked, "Why couldn't we drive out the spirit?" He replied, "Because you have so little faith. Truly I tell you, if you have faith as small as a mustard seed, you can say to this mountain, 'Move from here to there,' and it will move. Nothing will be impossible for you."*

Faith is like a muscle that we exercise daily and the more we use it, the stronger and the more mature we become. The Holy Spirit helps us with that growth. When the Holy Spirit came, the disciples took on a whole new level of faith and were able to see the power-gifts in action through their lives.

Those with the Gift of Faith believe God can and will do anything and everything. They sincerely believe that with God, all things are possible. If you want to grow in faith or have a hunger for this extraordinary gift, study God's Word daily. In Romans 10:17, Paul said, "Faith comes by hearing, and hearing by the Word of God."

2. Healings: the supernatural power to restore what is broken -- mentally, spiritually or physically.

It is unfortunate that many people don't believe this gift is still available for them today. They proudly say, "Healing passed away with Jesus and the apostles." Well, I am living proof that they are wrong. My life is proof-positive of the wonder-working, healing power of Jesus today. Of course the enemy wants us to avoid praying for the sick and to merely believe, "Only, if it's God's will." That's a cop-out. It's a definite lack of faith and you will never see Jesus or any of the apostles take that stand in scripture. That is a perspective of people who have been hurt by death or who don't have faith in Jesus being "the SAME yesterday, today and forever."

It's easier for us to say, "Only, if it's God's will…" than to rise up in faith and take a courageous stand on God's Word to "ONLY believe." (Mark 5:36)

RAISED FROM THE DEAD

In my 30's, I was visiting my local library to check out a few books for my kids. When I turned the corner down one of the aisles, there was a woman lying on the floor. From all signs, it appeared she was dead. She was purple, not breathing and had no pulse. I screamed for help and asked for someone to call 911 for help. The next thing that popped in to my head was, "What if she's not a believer?" Then I prayed, "Dear God, please let me be sure she knows you before she dies."

I began praying in the Spirit, knowing I didn't know CPR and was the only one there at the moment. I rebuked the spirit of death and commanded her body to rise up. About that time, another woman came, who knew CPR and began to administer it to her. I continued to pray both in the Spirit and with understanding, quoting scriptures of healing with great force and confidence. The woman performing CPR said, "She's dead." I responded, "NO! Please keep going."

I continued to pray over this very lifeless body and then suddenly she opened her eyes and took a breath. I immediately said, "Ma'am, you did not have a pulse. Can you understand me?" Very dazed, she replied, "Yes." I asked if she had a relationship with Jesus Christ and with a tear running down her face, she said, "No." I knew time was of the essence, so I prayed instantly for her salvation as she held my hand and repeated the prayer. Then, she stopped breathing again.

The woman performing CPR was a Christian, and she was crying as she witnessed the moment. I knew God wasn't finished so I asked the woman to please continue CPR. She continued, and I prayed with great passion. "I command this body to live and not die. In the name of Jesus, rise up and walk." Again, she opened her eyes and about that time the paramedics showed up and took over.

After they took her to the hospital and kept her there for numerous tests, they said it was a miracle that I was in that aisle and took whatever action I did for this woman's life. They said that not only would she have died, but without oxygen, to her brain, it could have rendered her severely mentally and physically impaired. The woman lived and even started coming to our church to learn more about her new faith.

Where did this miracle happen? Was it in a church or another ministry event? NO! It was in a library, in the marketplace, right where we spend the majority of our days.

> God desires that ALL be healed, and nowhere does it say that Jesus simply prayed "If it be the Father's will", when it came to a physical healing.

3. Working of Miracles: the supernatural occurrence that defies the law of nature and cannot be explained other than it is a divine work of God.

An example would be the parting of the Red Sea for the children of Israel to walk across on dry land. Other examples of the working of miracles are many as we consider Jesus' ministry: turning water into wine, raising the dead, feeding multitudes with a few loaves of bread and fish. Not to be confused with healing, which is God's restorative power with the human body, miracles are creative acts that go against ordinary laws of nature.

We need an outpouring of miracles today, not because we, as believers, require a sign, but because the world needs Jesus and when they see His power manifested on earth today, it causes their hearts to believe and fear Him as the Son of God.

When the disciples were caught in a devastating storm, Jesus saw their unbelief, and so He walked toward them on the Sea of Galilee. Walking on water is a notable miracle. (John 6:18-20)

Throughout the Bible, we find miracle after miracle, and they were always to encourage people to believe in the power of God and His love for caring for His children. It was, and never will be, a spiritual vending machine or a means to only get what we want from God. Miracles are like lighthouses that point to the Father and help us know that He is in control. When a man takes credit for miracles or uses the Gift of Miracles for self-promotion, God always corrects and lovingly brings order back to the purpose of the gift, which is to bring glory to God.

For discussion or meditation: How have you seen the power gifts in operation?

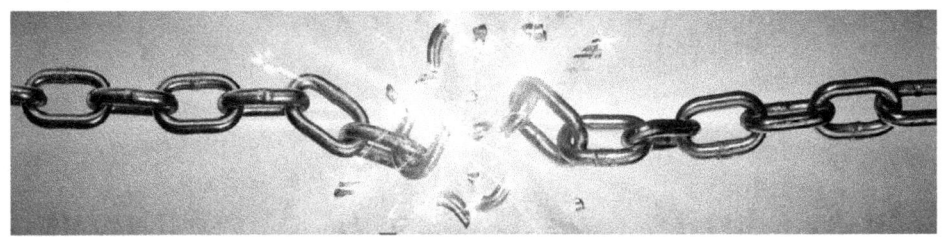

CHAPTER TWENTY-TWO

THE FINAL COUNTDOWN

Ten, nine, eight, seven, six, five… you are now in the final countdown for your launch into marketplace ministry! But, before you are launched, it's important that you recognize how valuable the gifts are that God has been placed within you. You are powerful beyond words and equipped with everything you will ever need to help those who are desperate for healing, salvation and deliverance.

The most effective way to be trained for any job, position, or ministry is to have a mentor or leader show you the ropes. I love taking people out into the marketplace, at restaurants, grocery stores or gas stations and showing them how easy it is to pray for strangers and invite them into a deeper relationship with God.

In these hands-on training and equipping classes, we have seen God perform radical miracles, heal the sick, bring freedom to lesbian couples that have renounced their marriages, and demonic spirits have been cast out of people's lives in an instant. But what's most powerful is to see the number of lost and hurting souls be radically saved by the grace of God simply by ordinary people sharing the Good News of Jesus Christ.

None of these people would have stepped into a church building but we met them in the marketplace. This is how we steward the gifts God has entrusted us. Ideally, it would be great if you could attend one of our "activate" weekends where we give you hands-on instruction in how to pray for people, lay hands on the sick, cast out demons and operate in full spiritual authority. But that is why I wrote this book. The next few chapters will teach you clearly how Kingdom stewardship works.

Stewardship (n): *the careful management of something entrusted to one's care.*

Everything in this life is an act of stewardship because everything is a gift from God. Our families, friends, relationships, cars, bank account, bodies and animals have all been given to us for a season and what we do with those gifts are our gift back to God. To be a steward of God's gifts is taking what He has given us and using them and managing them with intentional care and great humility.

> **Stewardship of God's spiritual gifts is essential in the quest to fulfill our purpose and potential on earth.**

The overall purpose for this book is to enlighten readers to know that they have been called to their job, neighborhood, school, church, civic organization, family and even their spouse to be a leader that helps others have a more intimate and deeper walk with God. Spiritual gifts help us to get the job done. God gives us specific gifts for our specific calling. Let's talk about how to receive the Gifts of the Spirit and what to do with those gifts once they are in our toolbox.

Before my grandfather passed away, I remember one day very clearly that impacted my life. He was seated in his favorite blue recliner talking about his toolbox. My head was gently resting on his lap when he said, "Staci, God has gifted you with a great calling that will require you to have a toolbox that contains the fullness of the Holy Spirit. There will be those who will try to convince you that you can only have one tool or spiritual gift, but they don't understand that God doesn't withhold any good thing from His children. A day is coming when you will need to access the entire toolbox of Spiritual Gifts. Yes, you will have a specific gift that is most powerful in your life. But my dear, God has given you an entire toolbox of gifts that are at your disposal. On one day He may ask you to lay hands on the sick and you will need to pull out that "hammer" and pray for healing. Another day, He may use you to speak to nations with the Gift of Prophecy and you will pull out a "saw" and cut through the atmosphere of disbelief. You will not be restricted in the gifts because your toolbox is full. Be confident in this that God is doing a new thing in you and it is for His glory."

Papaw was so correct in his vision for my life. While I have specific gifts that are more prominent than others, God gives us all access to use the full toolbox when needed. Jesus and the disciples gave full proof of this throughout the Word of God. It is up to us to hunger and pray for the gifts to be accessible in our lives and then we must practice using them in our home, at work, in church and whenever He gives us opportunity to do so.

So, how does our toolbox get loaded with spiritual gifts? First, know that you don't "get" gifts, you simply receive them. To "get" means "to obtain by struggle and forced effort." God's gifts are not by our will but the Father's and when He gives them, they come freely to those who earnestly hunger and pray for them with a heart's intent to encourage the Body of Christ and point to God in all things.

PRAY THIS PRAYER

"Holy Spirit, I adore You. I earnestly hunger to be the person You want me to be and operate in the spiritual gifts you have for my life.

For the Gift of Wisdom, I pray that I might know the will of the Father and share it openly with those in need.

For the Gift of Knowledge, I pray that You would give me the mind of Christ so that I might read Your Word and fully grasp its meaning beyond my own understanding.

For the Gift of Discernment, I pray that You would let me see what You see and hear what You hear so that I can rightly divide truth from error.

For the Gift of Tongues, I pray that I may yield my lips to Your Spirit so that YOU can be heard by unbelievers in a language they know so they believe in You as the only and all-powerful God.

For the Gift of Interpretation, I pray that You guide me to translate heavenly messages clearly, so all can understand what You are saying today.

For the Gift of Prophecy, I pray that I might perceive heavenly revelation of things to come for the purpose of edifying and exhorting others.

For the Gift of Faith, I most earnestly pray that I would be filled with a supernatural belief and confidence in Your Word. When You call upon me to partner with You in the impossible, may I stand with unyielding faith and a blessed assurance that what You say can and will happen.

For the Gift of Healing, I pray that my hands and voice might be the instruments of Your restorative nature to those who are suffering physically, emotionally, mentally and spiritually.

For the Gift of Miracles, I pray that You would use me as the conduit of Your miracle working power on earth so that many will believe You are the only One and true God. Thank you, Father, for the privilege of receiving these gifts. I am humbled as Your servant and committed to using them only for your purpose to equip, enlighten and edify those You send my way. I ask this in Jesus' mighty name. Amen."

These are the nine Spiritual gifts Paul taught the Church in 1 Corinthians 12:4-11. He was passionately trying to help the people mature in their role as Ambassadors in the Kingdom of God. These nine gifts were for the purpose of equipping God's people in the ministry of taking the Gospel of the Kingdom of God to the marketplace.

In Romans 12:4-8 we see Paul, once again, trying to unify the people by explaining to them that they are the body of Christ. He explained that each person is like a different part of the body and so each one will serve a specific role by the grace of God. We call these the "grace-gifts."

The Grace Gifts

Romans 12:4-8 – *"For just as each of us has one body with many members, and these members do not all have the same function, so in Christ we, though many, form one body, and each member belongs to all the others. We have different gifts, according to the grace given to each of us. If your gift is prophesying, then **prophesy** in accordance with your faith; if it is **serving**, then serve; if it is teaching, then **teach**; if it is to encourage, then give **encouragement**; if it is giving, then **give** generously; if it is to **lead**, do it diligently; if it is to show **mercy**, do it cheerfully."*

Another way to look at the gifts of the Spirit is to see them as the culture of Heaven on Earth. As you look over the many gifts, you will see Jesus in each of them. He demonstrated to us how to operate fullying in the power of the Holy Spirit and how to be a perfect representation of the Kingodm of God.

As you begin to crave or hunger for certain gifts in your life, study them, find mentors who share in them. Ask God to reveal them to you and give you opportunities to use them in the marketkplace. Then, be prepared to step out in obedience to put the gift into action. It will require you to step out of your comfort zone. The more you do, the more you will reflect the Kingdom's culture, characteristics, and power to the people around you.

For discussion or meditation: What gifts of the Spirit do you see naturally in your life? Which gifts do hunger for in the future?

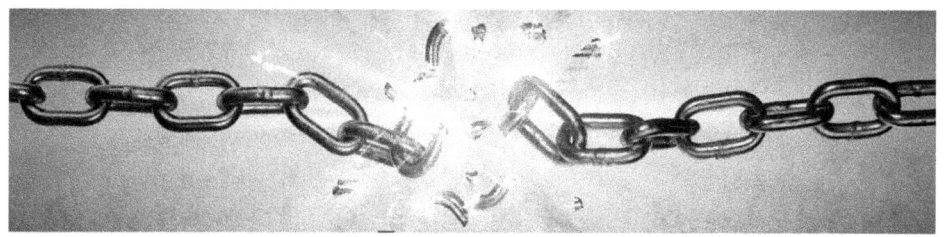

CHAPTER TWENTY-THREE

HEALING 101

*"When evening had come, they brought to Him many who were demon-possessed. And He cast out the spirits with a word and **healed all** who were sick."* **Matthew 8:16**

Everywhere Jesus went, He was setting an example for His disciples to follow His lead. He spent three years schooling His twelve marketplace understudies. He put them through a full immersion "how to" class on the ins and outs of healing, miracles, and how to sharpen their people skills so they could create greater impact. He gave examples on how to be effective communicators, listeners and He challenged His disciples to consider their words carefully so that they could have the same explosive impact He had on His listeners.

Jesus was very clear in teaching marketplace relevance and impact. Of the many healings performed by Jesus, only three of them took place in a temple or synagogue. The majority of the notable miracles Christ performed with His disciples were on the streets, in fields, homes, and in the marketplace. Jesus was making a point that He would no longer be confined by religious traditions or institutions. He wanted His spirit manifesting miracles in the everyday lives of people like you and me.

SLOW LEARNERS

Despite watching Jesus perform astounding signs and wonders on a daily basis, His disciples were slow learners. They couldn't seem to grasp the big picture of what Jesus was wanting to duplicate through them. Perhaps it was because they had been mentally programmed to only know God through a building or religious ceremony. Can you imagine how frustrating it must have been to be Jesus healing the multitudes, feeding the hungry, raising the dead, turning water into wine, and casting out devils, and yet even His very closest friends, His disciples, were like twelve deer staring into headlights? Throughout His life and even beyond his resurrection, Jesus' own "Dream Team," were clueless about what Jesus was showing them they could do.

In John 14:4 Jesus said to them, "And now you know where I am going and how to get there." Thomas spoke up and said, "No, we don't! We haven't any idea where You are going, so how can we know the way?"

OH, MY GOODNESS. I can imagine Jesus' thinking to Himself, "Dear God, are You for real? Is this the "sales team" you have chosen to duplicate My brand for eternity? Is this the best You could give me? Please let me trade in this team for a new one or at least may I please fire them ALL and start over?"

But instead of responding like most of us would, Jesus continued patiently with Thomas saying, "I am the Way—and the Truth and the Life. No one can get to the Father except through Me. If you had known who I am, then you would have known who my Father is. From now on you know Him—and have seen Him!" (vs.6) Then, Philip throws Jesus over the edge by saying, "Okay Sir, just show us the Father, and we will be satisfied."

Now, at this point in His attempt to get through the apathy of His "sales team," Jesus seemed to have grown deeply frustrated and said, (vs.9) "Do you not know who I am, Philip, even after all this time I have been with you?" He goes on to say, "If you don't believe what I am saying, do you not at least believe because of the many miracles you have seen me do?"

Then, like a seasoned coach in a pre-game locker room chat, Jesus said, "In solemn truth I tell you, anyone believing in Me shall do the same miracles I have done, and even greater ones because I am going to be with the Father. You can ask Him for anything, using My name, and I will do it, for this will bring praise to the Father because of what I, the Son, will do for you. Yes, ask anything, using My name, and I will do it!" (vs. 14)

HEALING SCHOOL

Today, there are millions of people that know of the many miracles that Jesus performed, but they are still like the disciples before receiving the Holy Spirit. They are thick headed and can't seem to believe that miracles and healing could flow in and through them to others. You, however, are reading this book because the Father wants you to experience the Holy Spirit's power for your family, co-workers and community.

The methods Jesus and the apostles used to heal the sick were many, and they varied with each recipient. However, the principles of healing were always the same and will need to be the foundation for how you pray for others as well.

1. Jesus was moved by compassion. Compassion was His driving motivator for every person He healed and the notable miracles that He performed. (Matthew 9:35-36) To operate in the Gift of Healing, you must have a heart of mercy and compassion for others. There is no place for ego or pride when it comes to being a conduit of God's healing power. Healing is not for your benefit or notoriety but for the sick to be well, so they can boast of God's greatness on earth.

2. Jesus treated the sick, even the outcast and unclean with dignity and respect. Whether it was the woman who was unclean and suffering from an issue of blood for 12 years (Luke 8:43-48) or the lepers whom others would not even go near, Jesus healed them all and had mercy upon them both physically and spiritually.

Matthew 8:2-3 - *"A man with leprosy came and knelt before Jesus and said, 'Lord, if you are willing, you can make me clean.' Jesus reached out his hand and touched the man. 'I am willing,' he said. 'Be clean!' Immediately he was cleansed of his leprosy."*

3. Jesus is no respecter of persons. He wants everyone to be healed, not just a select few. When you come across people suffering at work or in the marketplace you don't have to question, "I wonder if it's God's will for them to be healed." Jesus made it VERY clear that He wanted all to receive heaven's healing touch on earth. That is why Jesus healed ALL who were sick around Him.

Matthew 14:14 (TPT) - *"So when Jesus landed, he had a huge crowd waiting for him. Seeing so many people, his heart was deeply moved with compassion for them, so he healed all the sick who were in the crowd."*

Mark 6:56 - *"Wherever He entered, into villages, cities, or the country, they laid the sick in the marketplaces, and begged Him that they might touch the hem of His garment. And as many as touched Him were made well."*

Luke 6:19 (ASV) - *"And the whole multitude sought to touch Him, for power went out from Him and healed them all."*

4. Jesus has given you the power to do what He did and even more!
After Jesus died and went to heaven to be with His Father, He sent the Holy Spirit to empower us, His people, to finish what He started.

Luke 9:1 (ESV) - *"Then He called His twelve disciples together and gave them power and authority over all demons, and to cure diseases."*

John 14:12 (NKJV) - *"Most assuredly, I say to you, he who believes in Me, the works that I do he will also do; and greater works than these he will do, because I go to My Father."*

Who did Jesus say would do the work of healing and miracles? "He who believes." That means you and me and anyone who chooses to believe that the Gift of Healing is alive and in operation today. That means that instead of looking for a move of God, it's time to recognize that YOU ARE A MOVE OF GOD and He wants to use YOU to bring His healing virtue to the people in your workplace and community.

Thermometer or thermostat? Have you ever walked into a room and immediately known that the emotional temperature wasn't quite right? Perhaps you noticed someone angry or even in physical pain nearby. You may have walked past them "reading them like a thermometer" but not doing anything about it. In this new season, the Holy Spirit will begin to prompt you to shift the atmosphere like a thermostat that creates change. God wants you to be the catalyst of change in people's lives by praying for those you see in need.

Of course, there is a right and wrong way to do this, especially as it relates to your place of work. But don't be afraid, Holy Spirit will give you wisdom and instruct you, person by person, on how to be His hands, voice and feet right where you are. Soon, you will see that this is a powerful part of your walk with God and your obedience to His Word.

9 STEPS OF HEALING PRAYER

1.   **IDENTIFY:** Identify the person you feel called to pray for by asking God for direction. Then, go to them with compassion and create a connection. Personally, I like to simply tell them that I felt like God had laid them on my heart and then ask, "Do you mind if I say a prayer for you today?" Be sensitive to their personality and demeanor.

2.   **ASK:** If they say, "yes", ask them if they have a specific need you can pray for. If they are sick or in pain you could say, "Do you have pain or discomfort in your body right now? On a scale of 1-10, how would you describe your pain level?

3.   **CONNECT**: In an appropriate manner, ask if you can place your hand on their shoulder or hold their hands while you pray.

4.   **INVITE HOLY SPIRIT:** Invite the presence of the Holy Spirit by saying, "Holy Spirit, I ask you to come now in the name of Jesus. We thank you for your power to heal and restore."

5.   **LISTEN:** Pause for a moment to wait on the Holy Spirit's leading to see if He wants to reveal anything about the person's life to you. You may also want to pray in the Spirit to see if He gives you a word of wisdom for that person.

6. **PRAY WITH BOLDNESS IN THE NAME OF JESUS:** "In the name of Jesus, receive your healing. Be whole and free from all sickness, pain, and disease. We command all pain to leave this body NOW and we declare total freedom through the power of the Holy Spirit, in Jesus' name, Amen."

7. **LOOK FOR RESULTS:** Then ask them, "What are you feeling right now? Do you notice a difference in your pain level? Can you do something that you couldn't do before?"

8. **GIVE GLORY TO GOD:** If the healing was instant, say, "God, we recognize this blessing is from You through the power of the Holy Spirit. We give you the glory and we thank you for flowing through us today."

If they are still not whole, pray again UNTIL the miracle is manifested. This may also mean you need to continue to pray for them in the days to come.

9. **FOLLOW-UP:** Ask to stay in touch with them by getting their information for follow-up purposes over the next few days. Perhaps invite them to another time of connection, a worship service or to join you in a small group study.

Sometimes our prayers are answered immediately, and other times it happens over the process of time. Be considerate of the person you are praying for and continue to reach out to them, if possible. Once the healing has been confirmed, encourage the individual to share a personal testimony that can be documented. This is not for your own "bragging rights" but to point to God's healing power so others might believe.

Ask them if they have a personal relationship with Jesus. If they are willing, ask them to pray a Prayer of Repentance and Salvation. If you feel it is appropriate in the setting, you can also pray for the Baptism of the Holy Spirit. If they have never been baptized in water, make it a priority so that they can experience the fullness of their new life in Christ.

For discussion or meditation:
Who do you know at work or in your family that needs healing in their body? Are you willing to pray for them?

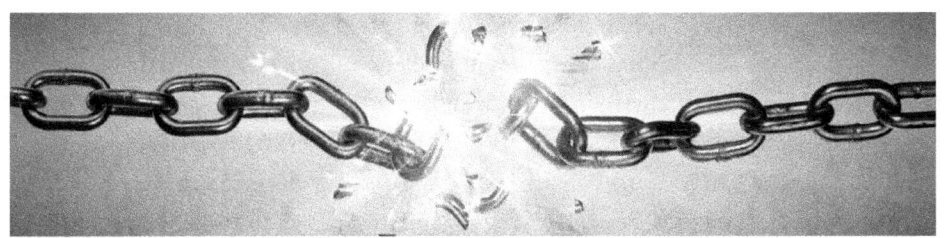

CHAPTER TWENTY-FOUR

BREAK EVERY CHAIN

Deliverance (N): *the action of being rescued or set free from bondage*

God not only wants to equip you with the faith to do what Jesus did, but He also wants to free you from the chains of bondage that have held you captive to all internal pain, shame and suffering. The Body of Christ is filled with people who have been redeemed and forgiven, but they still live bound to the sins of their past. While their spirit is cleansed by grace, their flesh may still be working through a deeper transformational process.

Standing in sharp contrast to God's plan for our freedom is the enemy of lies who lives to keep us bound to our sin and identified with our old nature. He seeks to destroy our confidence in being bold ambassadors of Christ in places of influence. Satan could care less if you succeed in your job or find success in your business. In fact, he loves promotion and wealth because he knows how addictive it can be, and how we will work our fingers to the bone to get it. The more we achieve, the harder we'll work to keep it. Promotions bring more work, tighter deadlines, greater stress, less time with family and ultimately leaves us with little to no time for being a threat to his kingdom.

Even the "busy-serving-time" we give inside the local church doesn't scare him. He loves to see us "busy" in the church as long as we aren't "effective" in taking Jesus out into the marketplace or effectively leading our families in righteousness. Satan doesn't care if we sing our songs and lift our hands, as long as we don't break the chains of bondage that continue to hold us back from being UNLEASHED and full of God's Spirit.

Unfortunately, today, there are countless numbers of Christians still struggling with their own sin and locked in addictions they can't seem to break. They love God profoundly but are bound by depression, anger, sexual immorality, anxiety and shame. We see countless leaders, CEOs, entrepreneurs, doctors, lawyers, coaches and athletes who hide behind their jobs, bible studies, social activities, acts of volunteering and other forms of busy work, while deep inside they suffer from the shame of past abortions, abuse or the pain of domestic violence.

When we repent and are baptized, we are given a new life in Christ. It is by grace that we are saved. That means that our sins are washed away but that doesn't necessarily mean that we are freed from the chains of bondage that attach themselves to our lives due to our past sin. Though the slate is clean through repentance, there may still be collateral damage or demonic influences that must be broken by the Holy Spirit through deliverance. Sometimes, those "chains" come in the form of oppressive spirits that linger with the intent to hold a believer back, or tie them up in bondage of guilt, depression, shame, fatigue, sadness, or a host of other emotional strongholds.

Case in point: One afternoon, I received a phone call from a precious lady who deeply loved Jesus and considered herself a devoted follower of Christ. She was calling for personal counseling for the deep emotional pain, anxiety, and depression she was still suffering from after her divorce five years earlier. Her husband of over 25 years had left her for a younger woman and she was still unable to forgive him. She regularly attended church and even volunteered there. Church leaders had prayed for her, but she was still unable to let go of the past and be freed from her suffering.

She openly shared her story with me and in tears said, "I just want to get past the pain and depression. Every time I see something in my home that reminds me of him, I literally feel as though I'm being punched in the gut. I have prayed and forgiven him, and I've even moved on and have a new boyfriend who wants to marry me. But I can't seem to shake the depression and physical pain. I cry all the time and I want it to stop."

As I listened to her, Holy Spirit whispered, "She is living in sin and has oppressive spirits attached to her life." I asked for permission to speak candidly to her. When she agreed, I asked, "Are you currently living in sin? I mean, are you and your new boyfriend sleeping together outside of marriage?" She burst out crying and said, "Yes. Oh God, yes I am. I know it's wrong and I know it must stop. I feel the shame everytime we are together, and I tell him, over and over, 'Never again! This is the last time.' But then when he gets romantic with me, I cave in and repeat the cycle."

I explained the power that sin can have in over our lives, and how it opens the floodgates for additional spirits of oppression. Then, I asked her, "Are you really ready to be free? Are you ready to break the soul tie with your ex-husband once and for all? Are you ready to repent, break the spiritual soul-tie you have made with the man you call your boyfriend, and become the woman of God you are destined to be?"

In tears, she said, "Yes, yes, I am. I have wanted to be free but haven't been able to do it on my own. I've been so spiritually weak and was searching for love and acceptance in my relationship even though I knew it was wrong. I have grieved over this far too long. I want freedom."

2 Corinthians 7:10 – *"For the kind of sorrow God wants us to experience leads us away from sin and results in salvation. There's no regret for that kind of sorrow. But worldly sorrow, which lacks repentance, results in spiritual death."*

I shared with her the story of Jesus meeting the Samaritan woman at the well who had five husbands and was living in sin. Jesus offered her freedom and forgiveness through repentance. She repented and was immediately transformed. We never hear of her going back to a life of sin, but instead, she became a bold witness and disciple of Christ. (John 4:1-26)

When this precious lady and I prayed together over the phone, we asked Jesus to be the living water she needed to never thirst again and to never go back to a life of sin. She asked God for total forgiveness and deliverance that day and immediately, those spirits left her and she was filled with the Holy Spirit. There was a physical change in the tone of her voice as she proclaimed, "I'm free! I feel it. I really feel like something just lifted off my chest."

One week later, she called with the good news that she had broken up with her boyfriend and told him that if they were to ever be together, it would be after a season of consecration, holiness, and right relationship with God's Word. She said it was the hardest thing she had ever done, but for the first time in five years, she felt freedom, wholeness, and an inner joy flood her heart. She said it was as if something had broken, and the heaviness that she had lived with for so many years was gone.

John 8:36 – *"So, if the Son sets you free, you will be free indeed."*

There is nothing more exciting to me than witnessing people truly set free from the grip of sin and death. When they identify with their new life in Christ and not in their identity as a sinner, they are able to experience the abundant life that God so freely offers us through His Son. We can attend our weekly church services, hear inspiring messages, sing our hearts out in beautiful worship songs, and still be without emotional, physical or spiritual freedom.

If there is not true repentance, the enemy knows we won't be a threat to his agenda. He will continue to pursue us with the intent to kill, steal and destroy our effectiveness as spiritual lights in this world. That is why Jesus sent the Holy Spirit. Without His power, it is extremely difficult to live free from sin.

Acts 2:38 says: *"Repent and be baptized, every one of you, in the name of Jesus Christ for the forgiveness of your sins. And you will receive the gift of the Holy Spirit."*

Countless Christians go to church every week who say they deeply love God but they remain bound by fear, pain, regret, sickness, shame and anxiety. It is not because they deny faith in God, but instead, it is because they have not been freed from the bondage of sin or the spirits that continue to look for entrance into our lives.

When King David wrote the Book of Psalms, he was a broken man, crying out to God for forgiveness. He loved God deeply but he had committed multiple sins that violated the Ten Commandments. This included his affair with Bathsheba, who murdered her husband to be with David. Narcissism, ego and self-gratifying lust seemed to have taken hold of David's life. Then, as we read the book of Psalms, we see David come before God as a broken and repentant man.

Psalm 103:1-4 - *"Bless the Lord, O my soul; And all that is within me, bless His holy name! Bless the Lord, O my soul, and forget not all His benefits: Who forgives all your iniquities, Who heals all your diseases, Who redeems your life from destruction."*

Brokenness and humility are essential keys to repentance, deliverance and the "secret sauce" to breaking free from spiritual oppression. Before Jesus multiplied the fish and loaves of bread, He broke them and gave them freely to those who would receive. (Matthew 14:19)

If you sincerely desire to be free from sin and *UNLEASHED* into your best life, you must give God the broken fragments of your past, repent and turn away from your sins. Then, allow God to restore you from the inside out through the power of the Holy Spirit.

King David cried out before the Lord in repentance and sorrow for his wrongdoings. He recognized that he had sinned against God and was in need of forgiveness, deliverance, and inner-healing. David learned through his own suffering, that sin not only violated his body as the temple of the Holy Spirit, but he had sinned against God, the Father, his most precious counselor, advocate and friend. (1 Corinthians 6:13-20) His heart of repentance led to God's declaration over David's life as being "a man after my own heart." Sin separates us from this type of intimacy, but what David's life shows us is that when we repent and turn away from sin, God gives us mercy, forgiveness and freedom.

The sad truth is that today, the world views sexual sins and biblical immorality as acceptable. They say, "It's no big deal….it's my body…it's my money, it's my womb…it's my life. I can do with it what I please." But the truth is, it is a VERY BIG DEAL and it opens our lives to strong chains of spiritual bondage that lead to oppressive emotions, soul ties, depression and anxiety. Sinning against God comes with consequences that always lead to suffering.

Even scientific research has proved that the practices of immorality most commonly supported today are harmful to our lives: spirit, soul, and body. The stress, anxiety and addictions that come with sexual sin, pornography, adultery, pedophilia, drugs, addiction, lying, cheating and basic violations of God's word have resulted in symptoms that often require medications to counter-balance the suffering that they create.

Look at the long list of warnings on prescription labels that are offered to treat the symptoms of anxiety, depression, sleeplessness, fear, heart disease, etc. According to the Washington Post, "The U.S. spends more on health care than any other country. Last year, we spent **$4.8 trillion** on health care -- a number so large that it can be difficult to grasp its scale."

What is driving this hunger for self-gratifying, power-seeking pleasures? This is not merely a battle of the flesh, but it is a Holy War pushing the agenda: to kill, steal and destroy God's people and wipe them off the face of the earth before they fulfill their destiny.

Perhaps you have struggled with financial issues for years, and no matter how hard you try, you can't seem to break free from the bondage of debt. Maybe you find yourself with a sleeping disorder, insomnia, nightmares, social anxiety or other debilitating mental health issues that seem to linger. While doctors may prescribe medical drugs to help you cope with the symptoms, true and lasting FREEDOM will only come by attacking the actual root cause or spiritual oppression through the power of the Holy Spirit.

Perhaps you've had an abortion, dabbled in witchcraft, been sexually immoral, played around with pornography or given precious hours to watching movies that contain clear and bold spirits of immorality, murder, adultery or other forms of sin. Seems like no big deal, right? Everyone does it, right? It's popular and acceptable, right? It might be what the world deems as permissible, but there is no doubt it is not beneficial, and it opens your life, your home, and your family to dark spirits of bondage.

God loves us SO much that He sent His son, not just to pay the price for our sin, but He sent His Holy Spirit to give us power over sin and a life of complete and total freedom.

To be UNLEASHED in the the marketplace as effective and bold leaders, we must be freed from the sins of our past so that we can experience the abundant life Christ came to give us. (John 10:10) Before you launch out to bring freedom to the world around you, let's make sure you have experienced freedom within YOU.

For discussion or meditation:
What areas of life do you still struggle to maintain total freedom and deliverance? Are they emotional, physical or addictive behaviors you want to break free from, once and for all?

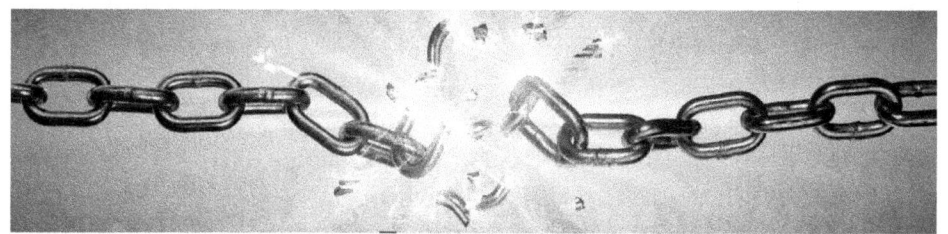

CHAPTER TWENTY-FIVE

THE JEZEBEL SPIRIT

When I was writing this book about being UNLEASHED in the marketplace, I had no intention of talking about deliverance, demons, sex or bondage due to sin. When the Holy Spirit persuaded me to go in this direction, I asked, "For real? Can't we talk about grace, joy or maybe the favor of God? Those topics sell more books and are so well received by the masses." But clearly God had a different plan. He wants us to experience the fullness of His power, deliverance, and freedom. So, with a resounding "YES", I am writing this chapter of the book to go even deeper. My husband said, "Honey, when you've gone in over your head, does it really matter how deep the water is?"

Over the next few pages I will unveil Satan's seductive mistress, sent to trap God's people in a life of sin and run out God's prophets from their position of authority. Her name is Jezebel and she is a demonic spirit that lingers on this earth, seeking to devour those who pursue God's purposes.

Ephesians 6:12 (NIV) – *"For our struggle is not against flesh and blood, but against the rulers, against the authorities, against the powers of this dark world and the spiritual forces of evil in the heavenly realms."*

Jezebel is one of the most obvious spirits unleashed in the marketplace, and even churches today. This is the same spirit of darkness that pursued the prophets in the Old Testament and defiled the sacred worship of God's people. It is the seductive spirit of Jezebel that has roamed the earth for thousands of years, manipulating the minds and emotions of men and women, especially those in places of power and influence. Jezebel thrives on human strength and ego and defines our popular culture today.

We first learn of Jezebel as the rejected daughter of King Ethbaal who was also the priest of the cult of Baal in 1 Kings 16:31. This wicked cult was known for its witchcraft, false-gods, human degradation, sexual seduction, the sacrifice of living babies, male domination, lewdness, hatred, narcissism and an insatiable search for power. Later, Ahab, King of Israel, married Jezebel and then, together, they led the nation into Baal worship, further expanding Jezebel's demonic influence over Israel.

Though Jezebel, the woman, suffered a horrific death, scripture tells us that the Jezebel spirit still lives today and lingers on earth to manipulate and seduce both men and women. As a spirit of darkness, Jezebel is not gender biased. She seeks to destroy anyone, male or female, who takes a stand for God. Tolerating her deception and making entertainment of her immorality clearly angers God and opens the door to great suffering and confusion. In the book of Revelation, John is speaking to the church about their sin.

Revelation 2:19-22 — *'I know your works, your love and faith and service and patient endurance, and that your latter works exceed the first. But I have this against you, that you continue to tolerate that woman Jezebel, who calls herself a prophetess and is teaching and seducing my servants to practice sexual immorality and to eat food sacrificed to idols. I gave her time to repent, but she refuses to repent of her sexual immorality. Behold, I will throw her onto a sickbed, and those who commit adultery with her I will throw into great tribulation unless they repent of her works."*

Think about our world today and the sexual sins, pornography, abortions, witchcraft, immorality, narcissism and manipulative spirits that permeate mainstream television, media, music and modern culture. Our generation has, somehow, embraced these sins as our new "normal". Their common appearance in award-winning movies and even commercials reveal how numb we have become to recognizing this controlling spirit called Jezebel.

While we have stripped our schools, courthouses and public institutions of any reference to God's Word and standards, people somehow want to blame God for the world's suffering. I often hear millennials ask, "Why does God allow human suffering?" But God is not the author of suffering. It is Satan who comes to kill, steal and destroy everything good that God has created.

God has given us the blueprint for a life of abundant peace, joy and victory. He has shown us how to live free from demonic spirits and the suffering they bring. Unfortunately, it would seem our generation has chosen, instead, to de-prioritize the Word of God and fall asleep to the lullabies of Jezebel's seductive voices. Yet, despite the way things may appear, God is always in control and He will not allow Jezebel to have the last word.

> Even now, God is raising up an army of warriors that are awakening in the Spirit, no longer hypnotized by Jezebel's lies and who are ready to wage war on enemy territory.

RECOGNIZING THE ENEMY

Perhaps you are struggling with feelings of shame, fear, rejection, exhaustion, isolation, depression, suicidal thoughts, drunkenness, anger, or sexual immorality. These are symptoms that may be the result of Jezebel's attack on your life.

Other signs of this dark spirit's influence can include prolonged or uncommon illnesses, near fatal accidents, a lack of sleep, sexually perverse dreams, a powerful hunger for control or a continual need to be affirmed. These are all indicators that you are being pursued by a Jezebel spirit that wants to destroy your effectiveness or disqualify you from Kingdom ministry.

Maybe you work in an oppressive atmosphere that has you under the rule of a narcissistic, domineering, manipulative or controlling boss or co-worker. Here are a few indicators that Jezebel is at work in the leadership of your company, church, home or life. (1 Kings 18-21)

1. People influenced by a Jezebel spirit play the role of a victim. They strive to manipulate others in supporting their agenda, even if it is contrary to the Word of God.

2. They believe that normal "rules" don't apply to them and that there are special "acceptions" for leaders of their stature or influence.

3. They surround themselves with "Yes" people or special layers of leadership who are willing to cover their impure motives or secret sins.

4. They name-drop, use flattering words, make promises and give material gifts to bring attention to themselves and gain more followers.

5. They are prideful, self-indulgent, and they love to bring attention to their physical bodies for social acceptance.

6. They believe they are never wrong and if you don't stay close to them or buy into "their way" of leadership, they try to convince others you are disloyal or unruly.

7. They are two-faced in relationships and tend to talk about others, hoping to gain trust with the person they are with.

8. They love to brag about their generosity and speak about themselves with false humility.

9. They are very insecure and do not trust the motives of others due to former rejection or past abuse.

10. They turn a blind eye to sin, witchcraft, idol worship, and sexual immorality because they are guilty of the same sins. They appear religious but are serving false gods.

If this list describes you, I urge you to repent and turn to God with a humble and broken heart. If tolerated, the Jezebel spirit will destroy ministries, churches, families, marriages and business. I recommend that you pursue deliverance immediately. Larry and I have dedicated our lives to this cause, and it is why we give such great time and attention to our counselling and consulting practices. More than helping people build great businesses, we are called to empower leaders to raise up Kingdom-focused families, teams, marriages and to clean up the Church also known as the Bride of Christ.

If this list describes your boss, employer, church leaders or someone in authority over you, the best choice may be to seek a new environment. If you feel led to stay, PRAY earnestly for their salvation and find other co-workers or people of faith to stand in agreement with you for their deliverance. Remember, this is a spiritual battle and can only be won through the power of the Holy Spirit.

But you might be saying, "Well, Staci, name-dropping, self-promotion, giveaways, social bragging, generosity campaigns and a search for followers sound like today's top marketing strategies for online growth. These are the necessities for being 'liked' in the world of marketing."

While that is true, if you are spending more time repping a brand that points to you or a company that stands in contrast to God's Word, you are being manipulated by a Jezebel spirit. Our lives and even our motives should point back to our heavenly Father. This is the example Jesus so clearly set in John 12:49.

Jesus taught us how to point back to God in all things. God wants the praise. God wants the air-time. God wants "our brand" to reflect His Kingdom online, offline, on the field, at school, throughout the marketplace and in our everyday lives.

If we were to go to your Facebook or Instagram account, who or what would we see you most representing? Would we find a reflection of God's Word and messages of His truth, or would we merely find YOU on display, supporting brands that stand in clear contrast to God's Word? Are you searching for God's approval or the public approval of man?

If we were to follow your everyday, normal life behaviors, would we see and hear righteousness, holiness and efforts to make God's name great? Would your body, mind and talents be seen as pointing back to God, the

Father? Or is your time being most spent creating a personal brand and self-gratifying empire?

1 Corinthians 6:19-20 - *"You are not your own; you were bought at a price."*

God wants you to have fame, not so that YOUR name will be great, but so that you will use your talents, business, and giftings to make HIS name great in all the earth. If the real promotion points back to Him, then your motives are pure. But Jezebel loves to twist our good ideas, steal our attention and turn our schedule into a manipulative use of time that leads to idol worship, earthly applause, and selfish gain.

Here is the good news. The fact that you have continued to read this book, even after this in-your-face chapter, means that you are craving more than mere surface Christianity. Holy Spirit is drawing you into a tighter relationship with Him. Perhaps, you have grown dissatisfied with the world around you and you know that God is setting you up to be UNLEASHED for something greater.

Even as I write this, I don't know who you are, but I know God is drawing you into a deeper and more exciting life than ever before. If you say "YES" to righteousness, repentance and the pursuit of God, you are about to experience the most radical, risky, reckless, yet real, relevant, indescribable and magnificent kind-of-love you've ever known. Jezebel will never be able to offer you what God has already prepared for you to receive.

For discussion or meditation:
Do you recognize the influence of the Jezebel spirit in your life or in your place of business?

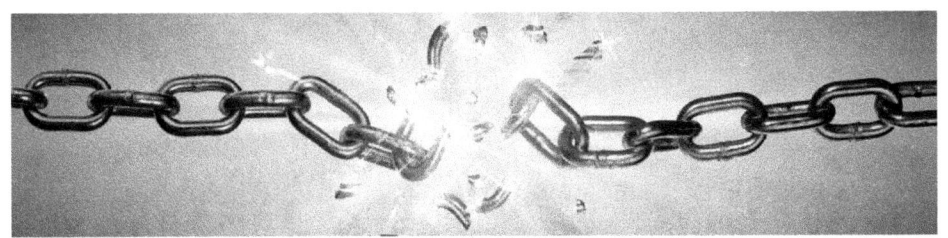

CHAPTER TWENTY-SIX

DELIVERANCE 101

"These signs will accompany those who believe, in my name they will drive out demons…" - **Mark 16:17**

The purpose of exposing selfishness, greed, manipulation, sexual immorality or other forms of sin is never to shame us or reject us, but it is to free us to walk in the abundant and powerful life God has destined for us. Spiritual freedom is all about love…audacious, risky and purpose-driven love. Praying for the deliverance of others is perhaps one of the greatest acts of love given to us by the cross. God not only loved us enough to send His Son as our Savior, He loved us enough to give us power over the enemy through His Spirit.

Matthew 4:1 - *"Then Jesus was led by the Spirit into the wilderness to be tempted by the devil."*

Jesus was a living example of how to endure the temptations of the flesh and take dominion over the voice of the enemy. Jesus was tempted in every way to let His ego, pride, hunger and desire for power to be elevated above God. Even Jesus had to overcome the enemy by using the power of God's

Word to counteract the temptations of Satan. No doubt, you, too, will be led by the Spirit into wilderness environments at work, in your community, and even in your own home.

You may feel alone, isolated, or even empty at times in your walk with God. Those feelings are not so that you will grow weary, but so that you can put into practice the very Word of God that was sent to heal you, restore you and empower you to take dominion on earth.

Jesus was aware of the strongholds and power of the enemy in this life. He showed us how to resist the devil and force him to flee. But what happens when we don't resist the devil, but instead, we fall prey to his deception? How do we gain freedom when we have found ourselves ensnared by the enemy?

Paul spent considerable time in his writings reminding people of the suffering that comes from sexual sins, greed, selfishness, murder, false idols, and other forms of temptation. But he was also clear that God is the great liberator of our souls.

1 Corinthians 10:12-13 - *"So, if you think you are standing firm, be careful that you don't fall! No temptation has overtaken you except what is common to mankind. And God is faithful; He will not let you be tempted beyond what you can bear. But when you are tempted, He will also provide a way out so that you can endure it."*

Satan's first attack is always through temptation. But he doesn't stop there. He will become relentless in his pursuit to wear us down until, eventually, we are ensnared in a spiritual bond to his kingdom. For this reason, the ministry of deliverance is essential for Christians today.

Unfortunately, Hollywood has created movies like *The Exorcist* to hyper-dramatize the act of deliverance and therefore scare people from its importance in ministry today. There are even a lot of churches and Christians who think that believers cannot have demons. However, I have seen with my own eyes that a demon, though unable to enter a Christian's spirit, can flood their soul, including their mind, will, emotions and flesh.

It's hard to believe people could go to church on Sundays and yet practice various forms of witchcraft, abortions, addiction, sexual immorality and idol worship the rest of the week. But it happens every day and therefore it is risky business to play with sin that can lead to bondage.

CLEANING HOUSE

Mark 1:39 - *"And He went into their synagogues throughout all Galilee, preaching and casting out the demons."*

The three years of public ministry demonstrated by Jesus were to exemplify the life we should live in our own homes, churches, workplaces and communities. Jesus visited synagogues, not just to listen to a rabbi or minister tell Him how to live, but to cast out demons and declare the truth of His Father. He was consistently about His Father's business and used various methods of deliverance, including:

- "Go!" (Matt. 8:32)
- "Rebuked the demon" (Matt. 17:18)
- "Be silent and come out of him" (Mark 1:25)
- "Come out of the man, you unclean spirit!" (Mark 5:8)
- "You mute and deaf spirit, I command you, come out of him, and enter him no more" (Mark 9:25)
- "You are loosed from your infirmity" (Luke 13:12)
- "Unbind him, and let him go" (John 11:44)

Deliverance doesn't have to be over-spiritualized, but it should be a part of every believer's ministry in the marketplace. (Mark 16:17) If you see hurting, oppressed, depressed or sick people in your church, office or community, you should pray for them, cast out evil spirits and allow yourself to be moved by the Holy Spirit in power. To be *UNLEASHED and Anointed for Kingdom Business* means that you are going to do what Jesus did in the marketplace around you.

CLEAN UP, CLEAN UP

When my kids were toddlers, they loved Barney the Dinosaur. I thought we would never escape the Barney years and his mind-numbing songs that would play over and over in our heads. One of Barney's songs said, "Clean up, clean up, everybody everywhere. Clean up, clean up, everybody do your share!"

Before you launch out to clean up the world around you, take time to clean up the world within you. Look at these areas of spiritual influence and see if there are areas you need to clean up so that the flow of God's Spirit can rush through you without hinderance.

1. BOOKS AND MOVIES: One of the ways the enemy likes to invade our lives is through forms of "infestation" that come through the books, movies and entertainment we bring into our homes. This is a form of witchcraft that can be exposed to our lives through curses that have been placed on movies, animals, dolls, games or other earthly objects that have been present during occult activity. The world would try to convince you that there is nothing wrong with a good book of wizards, a game of Dungeons and Dragons, Ouija boards, fortune tellers, or a good flick on the paranormal.

If you have made these activities a part of your entertainment, you may have opened doors to swarming spirits that can cause physical disease, uncontrollable outbursts of anger, convulsions and heavy depression. If you own books, movies or idols from occult worship or that contain witchcraft or wizardry, remove the items from your life immediately, and command the associated spirits to be cast out of your midst, in Jesus' name.

2. IMMORALITY: Sinning against God is not just a choice to violate His Word, but it's an invitation to the kingdom of darkness to enter your mind, will and emotions. If you feel a sense of recurring isolation, rejection, hopelessness, despondency, depression, heaviness, discouragement or loneliness, chances are, you are being oppressed by the enemy with the intent to take you out of marketplace ministry. Check yourself for areas of compromise, dishonesty, immorality or unforgiveness, and seek forgiveness and freedom through the Holy Spirit.

3. ADDICTION: When repeated exposure to sin takes place, it opens the door to addictive spirits that latch onto your life both physically and spiritually. It is a form of bondage that ties you up with cords to the kingdom of darkness.

> **Proverbs 5:22** - *"An evil man is held captive by his own sins; they are ropes that catch and hold him."*

The word "sin" means to miss the mark. In archery terms it means you are trying to hit the bullseye, but you miss. The word "transgression", on the other hand, means to fall back into sin even though you know it's wrong. The word, "iniquity", however, refers to an addiction to sin that has turned into a chain of bondage that requires deliverance.

> **Isaiah 53:5** — *"But he was pierced for our transgressions, he was crushed for our iniquities; the punishment that brought us peace was on him, and by his wounds we are healed."*

Addiction can be formed through sexual immorality, drugs, alcohol, pornography, or other forms of addictive behaviors that are created when you open entrance to your body, eyes, ears or mouth. This can even happen when you sit addicted to a movie or TV show you know is filled with murder, adultery, fornication, or other blatant sins. Separate yourself from these things immediately and ask God for freedom, in Jesus' name.

4. POSSESSION: Possession is the most severe form of demonic activity. When an evil spirit has inhabited someone's life, it can take control over their body, mind and, in some cases, their spirit. This type of activity is not to be treated lightly, nor is it to be feared since we have been given dominion over these earth-bound spirits. However, it is a serious deliverance, and a God-fearing leader of right standing in the Body of Christ should be the one who exercises power over this evil spirit. Deliverance will come through taking supreme authority over the evil spirit by a command to depart in the mighty name of Jesus.

> **Mark 16:17** — *"And these signs will accompany those who believe: in my name, they will cast out demons; they will speak in new tongues."*

No matter what your past might entail, when you confess your sins, repent and are baptized, you can be filled with the Holy Spirit and cleansed from all unrighteousness. (1 John 1:9) As you step into this new season of spiritual dominion in your life, you can rest at peace, knowing that although the devil will never give up his deceptive ways to overtake the marketplace, YOU have been given power over him. Now is the time to step into your newfound authority in Christ and take back what the enemy has been stealing from you, your business, your family and the people around you.

PRAYING FOR DELIVERANCE

These steps can be used personally or when you are praying for others.

1. Repent: To repent means to turn around and go the other direction from your current course of action. It means to stop sinning and do an about-face towards God. This is the first step of deliverance and will result in a new hunger and pursuit of God, through the power of the Holy Spirit.

Acts 2:38 - *"Peter replied, "Repent and be baptized, every one of you, in the name of Jesus Christ for the forgiveness of your sins. And you will receive the gift of the Holy Spirit."*

Repentance is is the doorway to freedom. If you are seeking deliverance yourself, start by confessing any known sins in your life. Say, Jesus, I believe in your sacrifice to save my soul from sin. I repent today for _____. (List off any sins you currently have in your life.)

If you are praying for someone else ask them, "Are there any sins that you need to repent of today?" Let them confess as many sins as needed or as long as they feel led to surrender. Have them pray, "Jesus, I surrender my life to you. I repent of _____." Have them list their sins and be sensitive to their vulnerability.

2. Forgive: We cannot expect forgiveness, freedom or blessing if we are unwilling to forgive others.

Mark 11:24-25 - *"Therefore I tell you, whatever you ask for in prayer, believe that you have received it, and it will be yours. And when you stand praying, if you hold anything against anyone, forgive them, so that your Father in heaven may forgive you your sins."*

Ask the person seeking deliverance, "Do you have anyone that you need to forgive in your life?" Lead them in saying, "In the name of Jesus, I forgive _____ for _____. I thank you, God, for forgiving me as I forgive those who have hurt me."

3. Resist: To resist the devil means that we want his influence and powers removed from our life and no longer want to participate in His schemes, diseption, or tactics. When we renounce his influence, we begin the process of abandoning his strongholds.

James 4:7 – *"Submit yourself to God, resist the devil, and he will flee from you."*

Ask the person seeking deliverance, "Are you ready to detach yourself from spiritual forces of darkness?" Then lead them in saying, "In the name of Jesus, I renounce the spirit of _____ (list the names of people, games, books, forms of addiction, witchcraft, sexual immorality, etc.). I resist the devil and all of the works of the enemy from having control over my life."

4. Take Authority: Now is when you take full authority over the kingdom of darkness and its power over your life or that of the one with whom you are praying. This privilege is available to ALL who believe, and your confidence in this authority will grow over time as you continue to do God's work.

Luke 10:19 - *"Behold! I have given you authority and power to trample upon serpents and scorpions, and (physical and mental strength and ability) over all the power that the enemy [possesses], and nothing shall in any way harm you."*

To take authority over the demonic influences in somone's life requires a prayer of faith, grounded in the certainty that God can and will give freedom. Speak with absolute authority saying, "In the name of Jesus, I command all demonic spirits to leave NOW. We delcare FREEDOM from every stronghold of the enemy."

5. Give Thanks: Jesus was very clear that all miracles, signs, and wonders, including healing and deliverance, were for one purpose only: TO GIVE GLORY TO GOD. When someone is set free or delivered from darkness, it is imperative that you not take any credit or recognition for the event. Instead, turn the attention over to God and explain that this is the work of His Holy Spirit.

Isaiah 42:8 - *"I am God. That is my name. I don't franchise my glory."*

Pray this with them: "Father God, we recognize true deliverance is only possible by the Holy Spirit. We give you all of the glory and all of the praise for this day of celebration and freedom. Thank you for moving in our midst and confirming your Word, in Jesus' name we pray, Amen!"

FILL YOURSELF WITH THE WORD

Luke 11:24-26 – *"When an impure spirit comes out of a person, it goes through arid places seeking rest and does not find it. Then it says, 'I will return to the house I left.' When it arrives, it finds the house swept clean and put in order. Then it goes and takes seven other spirits more wicked than itself, and they go in and live there. And the final condition of that person is worse than the first."*

Once a house or heart is cleansed of demonic, the empty capacity must be filled with the Holy Spirit so more evil spirits don't return. The delivered person must fill their time, entertainment, and personal space with God's. It is for this reason that I recommend believers to engage in times of group worship, bible study, Christian counseling or Godly friendships that create accountability and impartation in this new life.

For discussion or meditation: What do you need to remove from your home, office or life that could be giving entrance to the spirits of darkness and oppression?

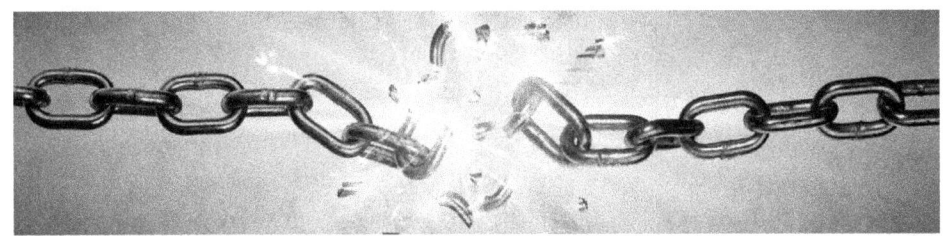

CHAPTER TWENTY-SEVEN

FINANCIAL FREEDOM

"For the <u>love of</u> money is the root of all kinds of evil. And some people, craving money, have wandered from their true faith and pierced themselves with many sorrows."
- 1 Tim 6:10 (NLT)

To experience total freedom as a marketplace leader and be UNLEASHED and anointed for Kingdom Business, we need to pause and cover the topic of money and how it impacts our decisions. Your relationship with money will either lead to freedom or bondage. If you see money through the filter of God's Kingdom on Earth, you will live a life of faith, generosity, and abundance. If you see money through scarcity or lack, you will live your life scrapping, hoarding, and gathering as much to yourself as possible. People with a scarcity mindset think that their success is determined by their bank account, size of home, model of car, or investment portfolio. It's such a limited mindset and it is the game of little kings who need to puff their chest with other little kings.

However, when you know who your Father is and the abundance that backs you up, you don't have to be prideful, neither do you have to worry. God knows how, who, when and where to bless you. He's your King. When you are truly free financially, you live in the secret place of the Highest Kingdom and hold confidence as a royal heir to infinite abundance. You don't have to flaunt it or tell other people about it. Humility is easy because you are fully identified as an heir of the Kingdom of God and you don't have to prove your wealth or status to anyone. It's engrained in you and so you steward it with humility.

You don't have to chase money, you just have to steward it. When you properly steward your Father's money as an heir in His Kingdom, whether you have a little or a lot in your bank account doesn't matter. You always have more than enough. You will have plenty for yourself and your family, as well as more than enough to feed the poor, and work as a change agent of generosity for others. God doesn't need a lot of money or material matter to make a massive imprint in the world.

Look at Jesus and how He took 5 loaves and two fish and multiplied it to feed thousands of hungry people. God didn't need the disciples to have a bank full of money. He wanted their faith and obedience. God loves displaying His limitless power by taking "nothing" and making something worth talking about. It brings Him great glory to see uneducated, unscripted, simple, and humble servants yield to His word and create a massive impact on the world. It's a principle of stewardship, obedience, and authority. How you steward what God gives you, whether little or much, will determine if you live under Kingdom abundance or stay enslaved to money being your demi-god.

MONEY ONLY MAKES YOU MORE OF WHAT YOU ARE.

If you lack integrity, more money won't fix that. In fact, more money will probably make it worse. If you have a drug addiction, more money will only give you access to heavier drugs and bigger parties. Money is never the issue to life's problems.

We live in a self-centered society dominated by a smoke and mirror effect. If you look happy, you are happy, right? If your social media filter makes you look young, you are young, right? If you look wealthy and flash the bling bling, you must be doing great, right? WRONG! Today's reality has been skewed by filters, AI altered videos, and selfie sunsets that makes everyone look as if they are living their best life. But are they really?

This generation has seen an all time high in depression, suicide, and mental illness. The drive for money, fame, and power has become an addictive drug that echos from the stages of hyped-up leaders sporting their multi-million-dollar homes, Rolex's, jets, and lavish lifestyles. They have lured and groomed a generation to hunger for riches but fail to teach the greater values of integrity, humility, character, honesty, morals, generosity, spiritual maturity, and true financial freedom according to the Kingdom of God.

Chasing money will never bring true peace and profits. Instead, it is like a bottomless barrel of endless searching for more. Enough is never enough. Money, itself, however, is not the issue. It's the spirit of greed and selfishness that sits upon money that creates an ensatiable hunger for more. Money, itself is amoral. But the <u>love or worship</u> of money can lead to extreme brokenness, confusion, ego, addiction, divorce, suffering and pain.

1 Tim 6:10 (NLT) - *For the <u>love of money</u> is the root of all kinds of evil. And some people, craving money, have wandered from their true faith and pierced themselves with many sorrows.*

Scripture commands us to *seek first the Kingdom of God and His righteousness and all these other things will be added to us. (Matthew 6:33)* Nowhere does it say to chase money. It doesn't say to strive or strategize how to make more money. Jesus made it very clear through His parables that money was merely a tool God uses to test our stewardship, obedience, and dependencies.

JEWISH SECRETS TO WEALTH

When I was 19 years old, I was the lead singer for a 21-piece orchestra in Canada. One evening, we were performing for a Jewish wedding reception when, on one of my breaks, the father of the bride came and asked to speak with me. He just wanted to know more about our orchestra which led into small talk about his love for old-time jazz classics.

Later, we talked about the Jewish faith and my Christianity and then he said, "You know the difference between you Christians and us Jews?" I thought he might be popping into a short joke, so I said, "No, tell me the difference."

He continued with all seriousness, explaining, "You Christians spend your hard-earned money wherever it seems most convenient. If you want groceries, for example, you go to the closest grocery store near your house. You aren't strategic in where you spend money. Your people scatter their money to whoever gives you the best deal. But as Jews, we believe in community and stewardship. In fact, the Jewish dollar, on average, touches the hand of seven Jews before it leaves our community because we buy from our own people."

I didn't realize the significance of that one conversation until it was brought to my remembrance nearly 30 years later. He was right. We spend our money at malls, in stores and online with little or no concern for who owns the store, what their beliefs are or whether they are building the Kingdom of God or supporting liberal, anti-Christ agendas. In other words, we spend, instead of stewarding our money.

We do the same with our time, our talents and our personal brands as we can so often fall into temptation to give our best to promoting companies, products and people that have little or nothing to do with the Kingdom of God. We scatter our seeds of greatness instead of strategically stewarding them into good soil that will bring about a healthy harvest.

Luke 8:4-18 - *"Jesus said in a parable: "A sower went out to sow his seed. And as he sowed, some fell along the path and was trampled underfoot, and the birds of the air devoured it. And some fell on the rock, and as it grew up, it withered away, because it had no moisture. And some fell among thorns, and the thorns grew up with it and choked it. And some fell into good soil and grew and yielded a hundredfold."*

Larry and I are extremely passionate about leading others into a life of personal and financial freedom. When we became debt free, our peace factor skyrocketed and our ability to hear clearly from the Father began to open doors that money could have never opened. We launched our consulting company, Fueled by Fire, with the mandate to partner with other business owners who wanted to know how to raise debt-free companies that create extravagant generosity for the Kingdom of God. Our company was about planting good seed in good soil so we could see a harvest of expansion in the Kingdom of God.

Our signature G.R.O.W.T.H. method teaches business leaders how to take their God-sized vision and turn it into a growth fund that feeds the poor, clothes the naked, cares for widows and orphans, heals the sick, and sets at liberty those who are captive. As leaders, God didn't give us the ability to produce wealth so we would live fancier lifestyles. Our success belongs to Him and how we manage, steward and distribute that wealth proves whether our lifestyle or His Kingdom matters most to us.

Psalm 24:1 - *The earth is the Lord's and everything in it....*

God is the owner of everything we will ever take possession of in this lifetime. He distributes wealth according to our ability to steward it and multiply it for His Kingdom. His commonwealth of distribution is not for our selfish ambitions but for His Kingdom expansion. When we borrow from banks or other people, we are no longer dependent on His Kingdom provision, but we become slave to an earthly lender and system. When we borrow so that we can gain more riches, we are not representing the King's culture or character.

KINGS DON'T BORROW…THE DISTRIBUTE

As Kingdom leaders, our hearts should not be set on bigger houses, more cars, fancier lifestyles, or deeper pockets. We should be following the New Testament model that compels us to steward God's resources for His greater purposes so that He gains the glory, and His Kingdom territory is expanded. It's a concept of stewardship over ownership.

STEWARDSHIP (n): *the careful and responsible management of something of value that has been entrusted into one's care*

From the very beginning of scripture, in Genesis 1:26, God gave humanity the spiritual mandate to steward the earth and everything in it. He gave Adam "complete authority over the fish of the sea, the birds of the air, the cattle, and over the entire earth." God gave man physical and spiritual authority, along with a command to multiply what He gave.

Genesis 2:15 (MSG) - *"Then God took the Man and set him down in the Garden of Eden to work the ground and keep it in order."*

Genesis is the first transcribed book about stewardship, management, process, and productivity. God was very clear that He was entrusting a wealth of abundance into our hands. Unfortunately, man quickly fell prey to Satan's voice saying, "YOU are more important than God's "rules" and if you trust ME instead of Him, you will experience true power and freedom."

> The temptations of the enemy led Adam to give up His perfect alignment with God in the garden due to greed and hunger for power.

Spirits of manipulation and selfish ambition continued to rule the hearts of man throughout the Old Testament, and they continue to do so, even today. That's why God made very clear laws about how to steward one's possessions, money and increase. God was testing the heart of His people to ensure they were not putting false gods before Him. He was testing the condition of their hearts.

When we are in partnership with God, our identity is in Him. His Kingdom is in us. We identify with His riches, His Commonwealth, and His righteousness. We aren't searching or striving for God's blessings, but we are living vessels of His blessings because the Holy Spirit of God lives in us. We are His temple, which has no lack or limit.

The floodgates of His abundance are always flowing through His temple, which are His people who are in right-standing (righteousness) with Him. But when we fail to put God first and be wise stewards of what He has given us, we are choosing to identify with the things of this world. We dam the floodgates of Heaven due to our pride and are we are left to what our mere human effort, striving, or natural abilities will provide. This was the summation of the fall of Adam and Eve. They went from limitless abundance to starvation and suffering due to their lack of stewardship.

KINGDOM DYNAMICS

Kings rule, reign and expand their kingdoms by taking over additional territory formerly governed or owned by other kings. They also ensure legacy and generational wealth for their kids or heirs. God wanted to expand the territory of the Kingdom of Heaven, so He created earth for Adam and Eve, to rule and reign. Earth was intended to be a perfect replica of Heaven where there was no sickness, striving, pain, or suffereing. There was only one rule set in place to be the test of allegiance and loyalty to God's rule. It was the Tree of Good and Evil. Adam and Eve were clearly instructed to avoid eating from the tree because it was a trap that led to separation from God, which came with shame, fear, greed, suffering, and isolation.

Unfortunately, Adam and Eve failed the test and gave the keys of God's earthly Kingdom away to Satan in the Garden of Eden. Instead of being totally covered and protected by Heaven's power and domion, they fell "under dominion" to Satan's lies, systems, and struggles. No longer were they provided for by the Kingdom of Heaven but instead, they had to work, toil, manipulate, and negotiate for their own money, provisions, and well-being. They had to sacrifice lambs, sheep, calves and other livestock as a way to stay in right relationship with God.

The rest of the Old Testament is the story of people trying desperately to regain wealth, power, protection, provision, and control of the things on Earth like money, land, possessions, people, and temples. Instead of being covered and provided for by the Kingdom of God, humans were slaves to the earth and its systems. No matter how hard they tried, they were not strong enough, wise enough or capable of taking back the territory and domion of what the enemy stole.

MONEY WAS AND NEVER WILL BE THE SOLUTION TO OUR FREEDOM.

People spend the majority of their lives striving for money, influence, and power but they are no better than Adam and Eve who thought the Tree of Good and Evil would give them the power they needed to feel in control of their circumstances. You can be around money, see money, and even have money in your possession. But when you CONSUME money in a way that is not covered by God's permission, you will become slave to it and lose the provision that only the Kingdom of God can provide.

That is why we read in John 3:16 that God so love the world, it's people, and His earth-territory, that He sent Jesus as a living sacrifice to regain dominion over the Earth. This was the plan to offer His people passageway back into the Kingdom of God and its total protection, provision, and peace.

When we believe in Jesus' death, burial and resurrection, we are choosing to denounce our citizenship of this broken world and regain Heavenly Citizenship as heirs to the Kingdom of God. When we do so, we also regain our royal inheritance, which can not be gained by skill, talents, human effort, or chasing money. It can only be gained when we detatch from the things of this world and reposition ourselves as fully dependent on the Kingdom of God.

Luke 4:43 - *But he (Jesus) said, "I must proclaim the good news of the Kingdom of God to the other towns also, because <u>that is why I was sent</u>."*

Jesus said that His #1 reason for coming to Earth was to share the message of the Kingdom of God. The Bible is a powerful constitution teaching us how to regain our position in God's Kingdom as ambassadors and heirs to His abundance. It is the contract or covenant between God and man and it contains two very important "terms" that we must comply with in order to expand His Kingdom on earth.

TERM #1: THE FIRST BORN

God gave Moses very clear instructions when He said, "Consecrate to me every firstborn male. The first offspring of every womb among the Israelites belongs to me, whether human or animal." (Exodus 13:1 NIV)

His financial expectations were outlined further in Proverbs 1:9 "Honor the Lord with your wealth, with the first fruits of all your crops; then your barns will be filled to overflowing, and your vats will brim over with new wine." God was very clear in saying that He does not want our leftovers. He wants to be FIRST in all things even as it relates to our disbursements of funds. By giving God our FIRST, we prove that we trust Him with the rest.

How does this apply to finances? So many people give offerings to God AFTER they have taken care of their own bills, taxes and desires. That's not FIRST fruits, that's leftovers! And it is not what God requires.

TERM #2: THE TITHE

Malachi 3:10-11 - *"Bring your full tithe to the Temple treasury so there will be ample provisions in my Temple. Test me in this and see if I don't open up heaven itself to you and pour out blessings beyond your wildest dreams."*

Not only was "first" important to God, but so was the tithe or tenth (10%). God was very clear with what the baseline of those terms looked like when He said, "A tithe (tenth) of everything from the land, whether grain from the soil or fruit from the trees, belongs to the Lord." (Leviticus 27:30)

God wants a tithe or 10% as a first-fruit dedication to His Kingdom on Earth. Giving a tithe and offering FIRST was merely His way of testing the hearts and faithfulness of His people to see if they would put Him in a place of top priority. Just as He told Adam and Eve not to eat of the tree of Good and Evil, God was testing their hearts to not consume what was His and His alone.

The fruit on the tree of Good and Evil was not inherently evil any more than money is not inherently evil. The curse fell upon their lives due to disobedience. They violated His instructions and sought their own will above their Kingdom connection. The first-fruit tithe, then, is God's way of testing our hearts and showing that we trust Him to be our provider. Instead of putting our faith in our jobs, our bosses, our bank accounts, spouses, or another source of earthly provision, our trust should be in God alone.

And why was giving the first fruits of our increase so important? Because, in Old Testament times, when you gave the "first," you didn't know if there would be a second born or more coming behind it. So, at that moment, you were giving ALL. You were showing faith that you believed God would provide more for you in your future.

That means you give your tithe or offering of generosity BEFORE anything else is paid. Fear or logic says, "Oh you can't do that. What about your bills? What about the rent? What about food? What about the concert?" But first fruits mean that you put God first. Not because He needs your money, but because He wants your allegiance.

God wants to share His abundance with you when you honor the contract and respect His terms and partnership. He can see if a man's heart is loyal by his willingness to abide by the Kingdom's financial instructions. In the same way, when we fail to adhere to God's financial terms, we open a curse on our finances that restrict the open flow of God's blessings in our life.

Malachi 3:8-9 - *"Will a man rob God? Yet you have robbed Me! But you say, 'In what way have we robbed You?' In tithes and offerings. You are cursed with a curse, for you have robbed Me, even this whole nation."*

I don't know about you, but I would rather have 90% of my income blessed by the Creator of the universe than to have 100% cursed by Him. Seems like a logical business deal to me. So why do so many people get offended or turned off by the thought of giving their money into God's financial kingdom? They want His support, yet they refuse to comply with His terms.

For discussion or meditation:
Do you think more money is the solution to your current challenges? Do you give at least a full tithe or tenth as a first fruit to God's work or do you give him your leftovers?

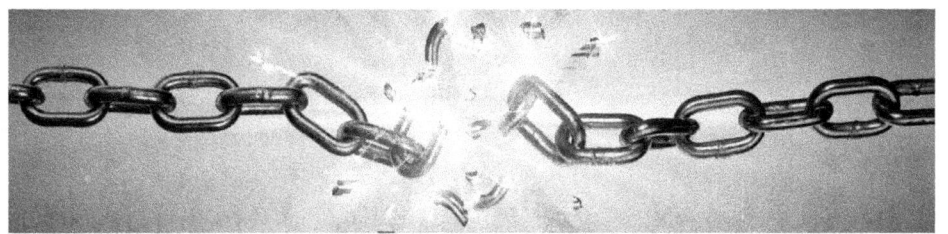

CHAPTER TWENTY-EIGHT

WISE INVESTING

My family of entrepreneurs used to love watching the TV show, *Shark Tank*. We enjoy sitting down together and watching ordinary people with a dream or product hoping to be approved for funding by such influential investors. One "YES" from the billionaire investor, Mark Cuban, could change their life forever.

Imagine this: You have a product idea that you think is a brilliant invention. So, you take it on *Shark Tank*. Let's say it's a revolutionary pair of sports socks, super-infused with antioxidant properties, anti-sweat, anti-odor and super-duper fabric that gives players an extra eight inches vertical jump in their performance.

You take time to get samples made up and do testing on a few teams, and you realize this could be a huge deal if you have the right investors behind it. You step on the *Shark Tank* set and begin to pitch your big idea to the team of Shark investors when three of the four tycoons shut you down and tell you all the reasons why they don't think it will work.

Suddenly, billionaire, Mark Cuban, sits up and says, "I like it. This is brilliant, and with all my connections, this could be a huge business. So, here's my deal. I will open my little black book of contacts to you if you give me 10% of the company for life."

Now, let's assume, Mark shared your values, would you want Mark Cuban as your business partner, knowing how many contacts, connections, and creative ideas He has at his disposal? OF COURSE, YOU WOULD! You would have one of the most powerful investors of our time who has more money than your little sock company could ever need. You would get to keep 90% of the company's ownership to run operations, build a team, and pay yourself a healthy salary. All Mr. Cuban is asking for for you to pay him is 10% to make it worth his interest and effort.

So why is it that we would give 10% to Mark Cuban without questioning a thing about how he would use it, and yet we refuse to give God 10% (the tithe) to be our partner? God has more access to unlimited wealth than Mark Cuban ever will, and God has a "little black book" that includes every human being that can fog a mirror!

It's insanity for us to rob God of His rightful stake of ownership in our lives by hoarding his 10% or generous offerings. Giving to God is not an obligation, but a privilege of partnership that provides us with a healthy and beneficial alignment with the one and only Creator of the Universe and His Kingdom.

Now, imagine a few months come and go, and suddenly everyone wearing your new socks starts to break out in hives with an allergic reaction to the fabric. Let's say sales drop drastically and it looks like you might lose everything. Do you stop paying Mark Cuban his cut because you think you need it more than he does, or do you honor your partnership and trust that the alignment is of even higher value than the company?

If you are a wise owner and partner, you will value your partnerships, knowing that companies come and go like the wind, but good partnerships are rare. That is why investor protection is so necessary in the real world. You can flop on one "big idea," but if your investors believe in you, they will support you in the "next" big idea. Why? Because they believe in YOU. They know you are faithful and just and their money is safe behind your leadership. Ultimately, your stewardship of THEIR money makes you worth the risk of investment.

Unfortunately, too many people have a hard time seeing God as their partner and fail Him in what matters most as it relates to financial prosperity and peace. They claim, "But tithing was only for the Old Testament. Jesus did away with that law." That is even crazier! Do you think Mark Cuban would wake up one day and say, "Yeah, so I don't want to hold a financial stake in your company anymore, but feel free to ask for my time, money, resources, and black book whenever you need it. I don't need your allegiance. Use me like a slot machine anytime you need me." That's a ridiculous expectation of any investor. In the same way, God didn't abolish His original contract with mankind as it relates to tithes and offerings. Instead, He sent Jesus to show us how we can do even better.

God doesn't change His ways…He improves His contracts.

A NEW CONTRACT

God is a powerful King and wise investor into the lives of His creation. The Old Testament gave us clear instructions on how to live, rule, and govern His people. The word "Testament" means a covenant, contract or agreement. People in the Old Testament failed to fulfill their end of the agreement with God. Jesus came to show us, by example, how to execute that agreement and fulfill it to perfection. Many think that Jesus came to abolish the laws of the old agreement, but Jesus actually fulfilled them and even upleveled the contract. (Brace yourself, this might shock you.)

Jesus didn't come to do away with the law, but He came to take it to another level of intense dedication to the Kingdom. Jesus explained the terms of the new agreement with His growing sales team (the Disciples) like this.

> **Matthew 5:17-18** - *"Do not think that I have come to abolish the Law or the Prophets. I have not come to abolish them but to fulfill them."*

Jesus was clarifying to His team that there should be no confusion on the new terms of the updated contract. The former terms were still in place, but a few "additions" were being made that would take their partnership to a whole new level of intensity that even surpassed the terms the Pharisees had to follow.

> **Matthew 5:20** - *For I tell you that unless your righteousness surpasses that of the Pharisees and the teachers of the law, you will certainly not enter the Kingdom of heaven.*

Jesus continued to explain the old terms of the agreement and how there should STILL be no murder, no adultery and yes, no robbing God in tithes. Each of those terms were still in place. However, to up the commitment, Jesus also asked us to go beyond those ideas to a more modern-day expectation of giving all.

NEXT LEVEL OBEDIENCE

Matthew 5:21 - *"You have heard that it was said to the people long ago, 'You shall not murder, and anyone who murders will be subject to judgment.' But I tell you that anyone who is even angry with a brother or sister will be subject to judgment."*

And look at how He re-addressed adultery: "You have heard that it was said, 'You shall not commit adultery.' But I tell you that anyone who even looks at a woman lustfully has already committed adultery with her in his heart. (Matthew 5:27-28)

Oh my! He went there! Jesus is getting real, raw and relevant with His crew. I chuckle when I hear people think that suddenly God woke up one day and decided to change His mind about His expectations of His people and financial stewardship.

Instead of lowering expectations, Jesus dropped the gauntlet on selfish ambitions and raised the bar on generosity. Jesus told him, "If you want to be perfect, go, sell your possessions and give it to the poor, and you will have treasure in heaven. Then come, follow Me." (Matthew 19:21) Clearly, the New Covenant didn't abolish the old terms. Instead, it intensified the agreement. As for the tithe or mere 10% expected by God in the Old Testament, the deal now.... Jesus wants ALL.

Not only did the 10% still stand as a baseline to test the hearts of the people, but the greater expectation was to use every part of their increase, their possessions, their land and their lives to ensure that God's people were taken care of, and His kingdom was advanced.

Acts 4:34 - *"There were no needy ones among them because those who owned lands or houses would sell their property, bring the proceeds from the sales."*

GOD'S FINANCIAL PLAN

God wants us to give generously and cheerfully based on our love for Him and others, not because of a rule-based Old Testament law. Many people refuse to give extravagantly to God's work and complain about the tithe or 10% expectation. But that was EASY compared to what Jesus was saying for today.

The tithe was the BASELINE, not the ceiling. Want baseline support from your business partner? Give baseline of your increase. Want abundance and open access from your partner? Give abundantly without limit. Want to be shut out and restricted from heaven's open windows of blessings? Drop below the baseline and put yourself first.

IF YOU FIND YOURSELF TRYING TO GIVE AS LITTLE AS POSSIBLE TO GOD, OR IF YOUFEEL UNCOMFORTABLE ADMITTING THAT EVERYTHING YOU OWN BELONGS TO HIM, YOUR HEART IS WRONG.

That is why Larry and I live to give instead of living to get more stuff. It's why we choose to live debt-free, owing no man anything but to love them. It is why our companies and non-profit organziations flourish and are dedicated to extravagant generosity. We wrote *Smart Money Makeover* to teach other business owners how to build a life and business without debt and how to give at least 10% of the company badk into the Kingdom of God.

We know that when we live with open hands, not sticky fingers, we allow God's blessings to pour through us. God knew "sticky fingers," and selfish ambitions would be an issue for man to grasp because it flies against every fiber of our natural being. It is also why Jesus had to lead a practical stewardship class every day with His disciples. He had to show them how to deny their egos and flesh-driven desires to show them best business behaviors and stewardship in the Kingdom of God.

Money matters were the topic in 16 of Jesus' 38 parables. Though there are only 500 messages on faith and prayer, there are 2,000 verses that focus on money and possessions. God knew that the love of money would be an issue for most people. Just as Adam and Eve succumbed to the enemy's ploy to trap them in greed, so Jesus watched the people in His time fall into the same bondage.

Jesus was very intentional with the words He chose to use, and there is one word that He chose four times in the New Testament as if to give His disciples an obvious lesson on the spirits that surround the things of this world. The word He used was "mammon," which describes a spirit of darkness that rides on the love of money and possessions.

THE SPIRIT OF MAMMON

Jesus never said money was bad. But He did clarify that our hearts would continually be pulled toward the spirit of greed that rests on money and seeks power or influence at all costs. That demonic spirit is called "mammon" and is what permeated the city of Babylon, causing it to be a stench to God's nostrils. (Revelation 18) God will destroy the spirit of mammon and every kingdom, government, and nation that has made it a god or priority.

When God was removed from our schools, courthouses and even the White House, not only did that open our children and nation to spiritual exposure and outside threats, but it also positioned our country in opposition to God. God will dominate the spirit of mammon but we, the people, need to be sure that we are on HIS side when that battle is waged.

Money, itself, is not inherently evil, but the LOVE of money is. Why? Because when we love money or what it can buy us more than we love obedience to the Father, money becomes mammon, a demigod or spiritual force of distraction in our lives. Mammon wants to replace God in our lives. If we become distracted by wanting more cars, more homes, more fame, and more self-seeking power, then the spirit of mammon becomes our master.

Jesus warns against it saying, "No one can serve two masters; for either he will hate the one and love the other, or else he will be loyal to the one and despise the other. You cannot serve God and mammon." (Matthew 18:24)

Jesus used the word "mammon" in His financial leadership class with His disciples because He knew the powerful magnetism of greed, lust and selfish ambition in the marketplace. He wasn't saying that you can't have abundant blessings or nice things in this life. But He was saying that mammon is a spirit of greed locked to this world that we must fight in the spirit realm.

THE WORLD OR THE WORD

The WORLD of mammon says, "Get, get, get!" God's WORD says, "Give, give, give." (Luke 6:38)

The WORLD says, "If they steal from you, sue them." God's WORD says, "If your enemy is hungry, feed him; if he is thirsty, give him something to drink." (Romans 12:20)

The WORLD says, "He with the most toys wins." God's WORD says, "Do not lay up for yourselves treasures on earth." (Matthew 6:19)

The WORLD says, "Push. Grind. Labor." God's WORD says, "Be still and know that I am God." (Psalms 46:10)

Jesus rewrote the manual on success in this world by flipping the mammon system upside down. You will NEVER have peace and mammon because the spirit of mammon consumes life and seeks to kill, steal and destroy God's peace and joy. You can, however, have peace and Kingdom profits because those funds are dedicated to God's purposes. That means they run THROUGH you versus sticking TO you.

For discussion or meditation:
How do you see the spirit of mammon in your own life?

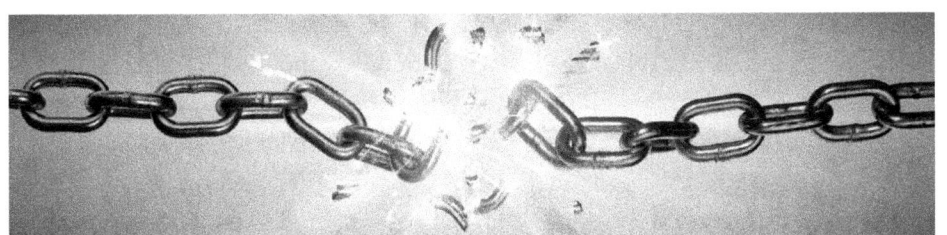

CHAPTER TWENTY-NINE

GO & GROW

To be *UNLEASHED and Anointed for Kingdom Business*, means that you, like Jesus, fully embrace your calling on earth to be ALL that God has destined you to be as a king, priest, and prophet. (1 Timothy 6:15, Revelation 17:14, Hebrews 2:17; 4:14, John 1:1) It means that you say, "Yes", to being a reflection and conduit of God's anointing and authority in the marketplace and world around you.

> **Revelation 1:5,6 (NKJV)** - *"To Him who loved us and washed us from our sins in His own blood, and has made us king and priests to His God and Father, to Him be glory and dominion forever and ever. Amen."*

Now is the time to stand up and step out with a boldness and authority like you have never known. You will be given untold opportunities to steward this privilege to those around you.

You may step into the breakroom of your offices and hear about a co-worker who is suffering with a migraine headache. You may be at a conference, and you may sit by someone who was recently diagnosed with a life-threatening disease. You may visit relatives to learn that they are suffering from anxiety or are, perhaps, going through a divorce. You may sit down in your seat on an airplane, and the person beside you appears stressed and uncomfortable.

In those moments, you will have a choice to carry on business as usual and stay in your own comfort zone, or you will surrender to the leading of the Holy Spirit and UNLEASH His anointing to the people around you. Saying "Yes" to the Holy Spirit means setting up your "marketplace pulpit" right in the middle of the real world and becoming the hands, feet, and voice of Christ. Remember, it is the Holy Spirit Who heals. That's His responsibility. Your responsibility is to merely be the vessel He uses to EMBRACE individuals at the point of their greatest need.

If you say, "Yes, Lord, choose me!", God will begin to educate, equip and empower you as His agent of change in the world around you. YOU have made it to the end of this book which has already defied the odds. Most people only make it through a few chapters before putting a book down. God has a purpose for this moment, right now in your life. If you close your eyes and say, "Come Holy Spirit, fill me to capacity," you will begin to know and tangibly feel His presence in your life. He will nudge you and sometimes command you to be His conduit to the lost and hurting people right in front of you.

> Being UNLEASHED as a marketplace leader, in absolute partnership with God, means that you are going to take dominion over the things on earth and duplicate His light, love and liberty to all those placed within your stewardship or sphere of influence.

It means that you love others more than you love your pride or possessions. It means praying for others when it seems politically incorrect. It means waging war in the Spirit when it seems that all HELL is breaking loose against your family or business. It means avoiding busyness to seek effectiveness that allows Kingdom advancement to take place. And finally, it means loving God enough to give Him your BEST in every area of life, including your finances.

When Larry and I realized that our influence in the marketplace was the very place God wanted to flow through us in ministry, we shifted our focus into becoming the marketplace ministers He had prepared us to be. Our lives and businesses became conduits of His presence to people we meet.

If He wants our money, we must have open hands to give. If He wants our time, we must stop our busy activities and live in the moment of service He is requiring. If He wants our leadership, we must be willing to step out in faith, even when it means going against the status quo and standing for righteousness. If He asks us to forgive our debtors even when a lawsuit is warranted, we lay down our right to be right and trust Him to provide what the enemy has stolen.

I will live the rest of my life writing about the miracles and how God has used our lives in the marketplace to touch the untouchable, reach the unreachable, and give extravagantly to those in need.

NAKED IN CHICAGO AIRPORT

I'll never forget the day I was returning from one of our national success events, flying home in my less-than-comfortable business suit and four-inch heels. We landed in Chicago and I headed to my connecting flight with my carry-on bag in tow. My plan was to get to my gate, check in, and then change into my workout clothes that I had packed in my bag.

I made it to the gate when chaos erupted. Out of nowhere, I heard screaming. I turned and saw a completely naked woman running down the terminal yelling, "Oh God, help me! Oh God, help me!" People were moving out of the way and acting like she had a bomb strapped to her body. She kept running through the terminal directly towards me when she suddenly dropped to her knees in front of me, threw her hands in the air, and cried out, "Oh God, help me!"

Without a moment's hesitation, I grabbed her in my arms and covered her body with mine. At that very second, something miraculous happened. As I held her in my arms, everyone else in the airport terminal seemed to disappear. It was as though we were alone. I whispered in her ear, "It's okay. God loves you and has allowed me to be here so that I can help you."

What was I saying? I suddenly realized the reality of the situation. I had just pounced on a naked woman in an airport with hundreds of onlookers. Now I am holding her in my arms, and if security shows up, I'll surely be in trouble. I probably looked a bit crazy myself as I continued to hold her in my arms and we walked to the restroom. A young man, along the way, threw me his shirt to cover her nakedness. Other judgemental onlookers just gawked and whispered.

Once in the restroom, she began to weep in my arms like a baby. She cried, "I am a bad woman. I have sinned." As she continued to beg for forgiveness, I began to share with her the magnitude of God's love. She assured me she was too great of a sinner to deserve access to God's mercy. I tried my best to explain the depth of God's love and that it was not by accident that she fell at my feet instead of a security officer.

She didn't know it, but she had run naked into the arms of God (or at least one of His vessels here on earth). God was using my voice, my arms, and my body to cover her and give her a message of love and forgiveness that day. She explained that she was grieving the loss of multiple deaths in her family within a two-week period, and she was on the flight headed to her daughter's wedding. Doctors had her on antidepressants that she had mixed with alcohol. Needless to say, her drug reaction, partnered with a nervous breakdown, sent her over the edge.

Shame filled her mind as she suddenly realized what she had just done. She had stripped off her clothes, stuffed them down a toilet, threw her shoes in a trash can, and dumped her purse in another toilet. She then proceeded to run naked down the airport in front of her husband and children, not to mention hundreds of onlookers.

Bad day? Absolutely! The interesting thing to me was that, during the process of her anguish, not one person stopped to help her. Not one of the other five ladies in the restroom that watched her strip naked said a word to her. They didn't reach out to help. They didn't even call the police. They just gawked in judgment and fear. That day, I learned a lot about myself, about God's forgiveness, and about human nature.

LIFE LESSONS

1. About myself: I realized that God allowed her to drop at my feet because He knew I would be willing and unafraid to reach out to her and give her hope, help, and healing. You see, God is not looking for perfect vessels. He is looking for willing vessels who will allow Him to use their life to reach out to others who are suffering in the marketplace.

2. About God's Forgiveness: I learned that God is such a loving Father who will do anything to get our attention so that we will seek His forgiveness. God watched as that woman took those drugs and drank the alcohol. He knew of her pain and sympathized with her sorrow. He also devised a plan for her salvation that included allowing her to hit a proverbial brick wall that would lead to her spiritual and physical healing. He loved her so much that although it took a complete breakdown, He got her attention. He walked her right into a plan for her complete restoration, peace, and healing.

3. About Human Nature: I learned that many people would rather gossip than help, offer insults instead of aid, and complain instead of complying with God's wishes to be a vessel of hope to those in need. As I considered how many people chose NOT to help that day, I humbly thanked God for giving me the courage to be different.

I genuinely believe that, for a few moments in time, God allowed me to feel His unconditional love pour from my heart and into that woman. It was a moment of divine stewardship and a beautiful example of God using the ordinary to do His extraordinary work on earth. I am wholeheartedly convinced that this is the will of our Father.

God wants our lives, our bodies, our money, our time, our talents, our jobs, and our hearts to be conduits of His love to the marketplace around us. When we surrender to God's perfect will, we become His hands and feet to a lost and hurting world.

As this book comes to an end, my prayer is that your journey of discovering the power of the Holy Spirit carries you on wings that elevate you into a heavenly place that echos with the sound of Heaven. I pray that you hunger and thrist to be lost in the magnificent presence of Almighty God and that you find yourself longing to be hidden behind His glory.

If you have fully embraced the teachings within this book, then you know you have been embraced by God, educated with His principles, equipped for His service, and empowered to go into all the world and share the good news of Christ with others. This is love. This is leadership. This is the blessed life. It's more than what we do, it's how we love God and how we should love one another. We can speak with tongues of men and angels but if we have not love, we are nothing but clanging cymbals in this world. (1 Corinthians 13:1) Be love. Be light. Be Jesus to the marketplace around you. This is what it means to be *UNLEASHED and Anointed for Kingdom Business*.

Matthew 5:14-16 - *"You're here to be light, bringing out the God-colors in the world. God is not a secret to be kept. We're going public with this, as public as a city on a hill. If I make you light-bearers, you don't think I'm going to hide you under a bucket, do you? I'm putting you on a light stand. Now that I've put you there on a hilltop, on a light stand—shine!"*

For discussion or meditation:
Do you consider yourself a generous leader of compassion? How could you be more like Christ to your co-workers or family?

ABOUT THE AUTHOR

Staci Wallace is the CEO of Fueled by Fire, a global consulting firm that helps CEO's, entrepreneurs, and thought leaders scale highly profitable, Kingdom-driven companies that reflect God's character in the marketplace.

For over three decades, Staci has been an Executive Coach, author of over 130 courses, books, and classes, and keynote speaker. She has shared the stage with five U.S. Presidents and other notable world leaders, specializing in equipping CEOs to recognize, clarify and fulfill their Kingdom Assigment while becoming conduits of extravagant generosity. She, along with her husband, Larry and children, Payton and Alexia, lead the global movement of Fueled by Fire, passionately taking the message of *Kingdom Stewardship and Authority* to the nations.

Staci and Larry are also co-Founders of Epiphany Global and EMwomen International (EMwomen.com), a 501c3 non-profit organization sharing the love of Christ to those in greatest need.

Learn more at:
www.staciwallace.com

To book Staci or Larry for your next speaking event, scan this QR code:

LET'S CONNECT!

Visit me on your favorite social media platform and tell me how this book has impacted your life!

Facebook.com/StaciWallaceOfficial

Instagram.com/StaciWallace

LinkedIn.com/StaciWallace

Resources

If you hunger for more wisdom on how to grow a life and business the Kingdom Way, visit **www.FueledByFire.com**

Our online Kingdom Alliance University model offers over 130 courses and mastery classes to support you in becoming the Kingdom CEO and leader God has destined you to be.

Scan this QR code to register for our FREE Wealth Mastery Course and learn how to build a debt-free Kingdom-Centered business.

www.ingramcontent.com/pod-product-compliance
Lightning Source LLC
Chambersburg PA
CBHW070048100426
42734CB00040B/2755